CEDRIC GROLET

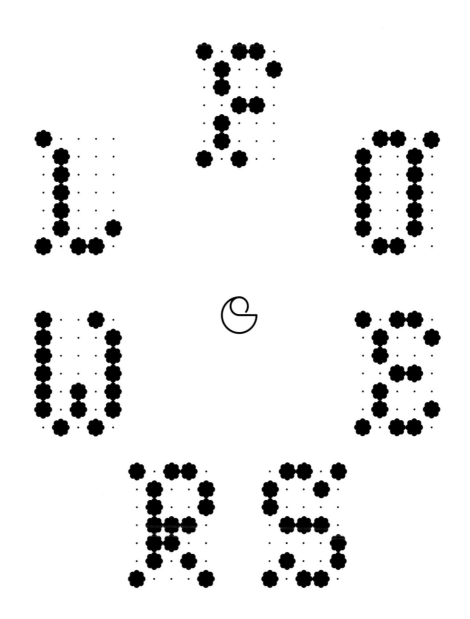

DUCASSE EDITION

AFTER FRUiTS, WHAT ARE YOUR PLANS?

"After *Fruits*, what are your plans?"

That is the question customers have been asking recently. And, of course, I answer, "After fruits come flowers." It stands to reason: Flowers are a beautiful subject, a limitless playing field for a pastry chef. They are a symbol of life, elegance, and purity. They provide an opportunity to play with colors, shapes, and ingredients. I find them exceptionally inspiring.

What's more, giving an edible flower is a wonderful gesture. A bouquet of flowers is traditionally gifted for a special occasion. I wanted to give this gift an added dimension by making it edible.

My first memory of flowers? I remember saying to my mother when I was a child, "I'd like to give you a present, but I don't have any money." She replied, "All you have to do is pick me a flower, and you don't need money for that." My mother's simple words have been so important to me; she was so right. I picked her daffodils and dandelions in the fields around our house.

That is how I came up with the idea of making cakes in the shapes of flowers for my shop, Opéra. I combined gourmet recipes with the artistry of piping. The recipes in this book need little equipment, other than a pastry bag and tip, and do not require difficult-to-find ingredients. They just require patience and a steady hand. It is advisable to start preparing the components on the previous day. Certain steps are long and some elements need time to rest, such as the ganaches, which must be chilled in the refrigerator for 12 hours before assembly and piping. In a way, this is the art of pastry: time, patience, and perseverance are key.

My first flower at Opéra was a flower I made out of Paris-Brest, the starting point for many desserts. With each creation, I try to devise original cakes using ingredients that are in keeping with the seasons, because my creativity is always guided by the raw materials. It is also possible to give tarts the appearance of a flower. It all depends on the consistency of the presentation, on the art of placing fruit in a rosette pattern over the tart shell. If the strawberries are too big or too small, or are different sizes, the result will not be up to par. The skill of a good pastry chef lies in knowing how to adapt to the raw materials available. The arrangement of the fruit is crucial; it turns a simple tart into a worthy gift.

Since my training, I have always loved to pipe. I was taught by my mentor Pascal Liotier, who I worked with to qualify as a pastry chef. He was different from my other instructors; he could be outspoken, which made him hard to work with at times, but he was also a wonderful person. It is because of him that I am what I have become today. I met up with him recently while traveling in the south of France, and he told me how proud he was of me. It was an emotional moment. He is an important person in my life, because he has shown me both his professional and human sides. I think we all need both of these sides to succeed.

"

THE ARRANGEMENT OF THE FRUIT IS CRUCIAL; IT TURNS A SIMPLE TART INTO A WORTHY GIFT.

"

I would never have gone as far with piping as I have in this book if I had not mixed up the pastry tips, the arrangements, the quality of the ingredients, the precision required by the creations. My teams and I made it a point to challenge ourselves. All the creations were photographed on pieces of ornamental plasterwork made by Atelier Louis Del Boca. The idea initially appealed to me, because both pastry chefs and the plasterers who create these works of art have a similar approach: We produce the same creative results. I like the idea of bringing these two crafts together.

Piping is truly one of the essential skills of the pastry profession. I have trouble when it comes to recruiting pastry chefs who can pipe well, because it is the skilled hand that counts—one that cannot be replaced by a machine. You have to be able to express your sensibility. Whether it is a Chantilly cream or a ganache, it is brought to life through the ingredients. I try to give shape to a flower, one that is different each time, by piping uniform curves. The rest is up to you.

CEDRIC GROLET

i'VE ALWAYS LOVED TO PiPE.

I was Cédric's mentor when he was training to qualify as a pastry chef. My first memories of him? His passion for the profession, his motivation, his involvement. He would practice tirelessly until he achieved a perfect result, for example, with sugar. He was always a hard worker; I sometimes had to take him out of the kitchen or he would never stop. That is probably what impressed me most about him.

Cédric learned to pipe with a Saint-Honoré tip in my kitchen. Every morning, I would ask him to finish off our Sous-Bois, one of our flagship desserts at the time that was made with berry bavarois and vanilla crème anglaise, and piped all over with Italian meringue. I used to tell my apprentices, "If you can pipe with a Saint-Ho tip, then you can pipe anything!" As with everything else he did, Cédric would never give up. He persevered until the end. To pipe successfully, you need what is called "a piping stroke," and he mastered it. Since then, his flowers, as well as his trompe-l'oeil fruits, have become his trademarks.

I remember that at eighteen years old he was full of mischief and had a zest for life. He had to be kept busy and given constant work, so insatiable was his thirst for learning. He was at the age when you discover what life is about. I have always loved being an instructor, and educator — what better mission in life than teaching young people a trade!

Since I opened my pastry, chocolate, and ice cream business in Yssingeaux twenty-seven years ago, I have always had two apprentices in my team every year. Passing on knowledge is a value that I love most of all. The relationship between a mentor and his apprentice is like alchemy, and, with Cédric, it worked perfectly. I immediately sensed the passion he felt for this profession. His talent has shone through and I am extremely proud of him. Since his year working with me as an apprentice, we have remained in contact. I told him repeatedly to stay humble and never forget where he came from, and he has.

Throughout his career, he has managed to find his own way, his own personality. By revolutionizing tastes in some of his creations and, in particular, by being daring—something that few pastry chefs allow themselves to do—he has succeeded in gaining international recognition and being named the world's best pastry chef. It is not uncommon to hear people say "That's by Cédric Grolet" when they see his pastries. Few pastry chefs can boast such recognition! Today, it has been an honor for me to write the preface of his third book. The student has clearly surpassed his master.

PASCAL LiOTiER

Cédric Grolet's mentor

CONTENTS

SPRING

BOUQUET

For the ginger ganache

5 cups (1.2 kg) whipping cream

⅔ cup (60 g) peeled and grated fresh ginger

1 cup (240 g) ginger vinegar (to make your own, reduce 1 quart/1 liter ginger juice to 250 ml/1 cup)

9½ ounces (270 g) white couverture chocolate, chopped

¼ cup (63 g) gelatin mass (2¾ teaspoons/9 g gelatin powder hydrated in ¼ cup/54 g water)

For the sweet tart shell

See page 342

For the almond and rose cream

4½ tablespoons (65 g) unsalted butter, softened

⅓ cup (65 g) superfine (caster) sugar

12-13 medium (25 g) crystallized rose petals (about 3 tablespoons)

⅔ cup (65 g) ground almonds

1⅓ large (UK medium/65 g) eggs (¼ cup plus 1 teaspoon)

For the rose water jelly

1⅞ cups (450 g) rose water

¼ cup (50 g) superfine (caster) sugar

2¼ teaspoons (6 g) agar powder

¾ teaspoon (2 g) xanthan gum

For the raspberry insert

3¾ cups (475 g) fresh raspberries

¼ cup plus 2 teaspoons (70 g) raspberry juice

2 teaspoons (10 g) rose water

¾ cup (145 g) superfine (caster) sugar

3 tablespoons plus 2 teaspoons (50 g) glucose powder

3½ teaspoons (10 g) pectin NH

½ teaspoon (3 g) cream of tartar

3-4 medium (7.5 g) crystallized rose petals (about 1 tablespoon)

For the ruby chocolate coating

See page 338

FOR THE GINGER GANACHE

The previous day, heat half the cream in a saucepan. Add the grated ginger and the ginger vinegar. Remove from the heat, cover, and let infuse for about 10 minutes. Heat the mixture again and filter through a conical sieve. Pour it over the chopped chocolate and gelatin mass, then add the remaining cream. Incorporate using an immersion (stick) blender until the ganache is smooth. Refrigerate for about 12 hours.

FOR THE SWEET TART SHELL

Make the sweet tart shell (case) as described on page 342.

FOR THE ALMOND AND ROSE CREAM

In a stand mixer fitted with a flat beater attachment, cream the butter with the superfine sugar, crystallized rose petals, and ground almonds. Gradually incorporate the eggs, then refrigerate.

FOR THE ROSE WATER JELLY

In a saucepan, bring the rose water to a boil. Combine the sugar, agar, and xanthan gum and add to the rose water. Blend, then let set in the refrigerator. Blend again before use.

FOR THE RASPBERRY INSERTS

Make preserves by cooking the raspberries for about 30 minutes, gradually adding the juice and rose water. Add the sugar, glucose, pectin, and cream of tartar. Mix and bring to a boil for 1 minute. Finally, add the crystallized rose petals. Refrigerate preserves until set. Pipe the preserves into 1⅜-inch (3.5-cm)-diameter spherical silicone molds. Freeze for about 3 hours, until set. Pipe a little ganache into 1¾-inch (4.5-cm)-diameter hemispherical silicone molds. Place the frozen raspberry preserves spheres inside and cover completely with ganache. Return to the freezer for about 6 hours.

FOR THE RUBY CHOCOLATE COATING

Make the ruby chocolate coating as described on page 338.

FOR ASSEMBLY

Preheat the oven to 340°F (170°C/Gas Mark 3½). Fill the tart shell with the almond and rose cream. Bake for 8 minutes. Let cool for about 15 minutes, then fill to the top with the rose water jelly. Refrigerate for about 30 minutes.

FOR FINISHING

Whip the ganache with a hand mixer. Hold a small (three-pronged) dipping fork in one hand and set a raspberry insert onto it. Hold a size 104 Saint-Honoré tip (nozzle) in your other hand. Pipe a tight ring of whipped ganache on the insert to form the heart of the rose, then pipe semicircular petals all around it, gradually increasing them in size. Slide a spatula (palette knife) under the flower to lift and carefully place it on the cake. Repeat the process, one rose at a time, to cover the tart entirely. Feel free to make flowers of different sizes to give the impression of a natural bouquet. Use a spray gun to uniformly flock the cake with ruby chocolate coating.

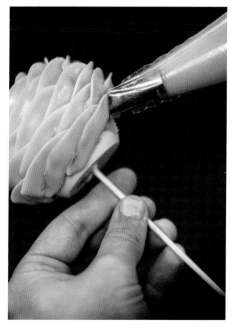

RHUBARB

PETAIS

For the hazelnut shortbread

●

7 tablespoons (100 g) unsalted butter

½ cup (105 g) packed brown sugar

1 medium (UK small/45 g) egg (3 tablespoons)

scant ¼ teaspoon (1 g) salt

1¾ teaspoons (8 g) baking powder

1¼ cups (150 g) all-purpose (plain) flour

⅞ cup (75 g) ground hazelnuts

For the hazelnut cream

●

4½ tablespoons (65 g) unsalted butter, softened

⅓ cup (65 g) superfine (caster) sugar

¾ cup (65 g) ground hazelnuts

1⅓ large (UK medium/65 g) eggs (¼ cup plus 1 teaspoon)

For the rhubarb jelly

●

1 cup (225 g) rhubarb juice (made in a juicer)

2 tablespoons (25 g) superfine (caster) sugar

1 teaspoon (3 g) agar powder

scant ½ teaspoon (1 g) xanthan gum

For the candied rhubarb

●

16 rhubarb stalks

18

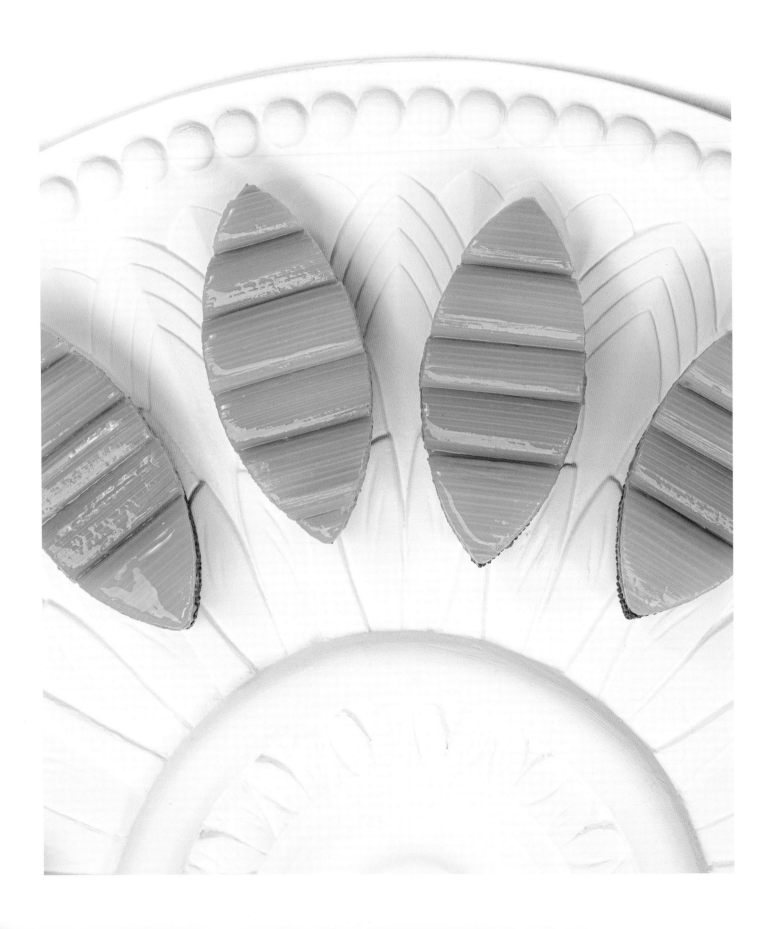

FOR THE HAZELNUT SHORTBREAD

Preheat the oven to 350°F (175°C/Gas Mark 4). In a stand mixer fitted with a flat beater attachment, mix the butter with the sugar until crumbly. Gradually add the egg, followed by the salt, baking powder, flour, and ground hazelnuts. Roll out the dough to an ⅛-inch (3-mm) thickness and line 3½-inch (9-cm)-long oval (calisson-shaped) pastry rings with the pastry. Trim off the excess with a knife. Place the rings on a baking sheet lined with a Silpat mat (or parchment/baking paper). Bake for 20 minutes.

FOR THE HAZELNUT CREAM

In a stand mixer fitted with a flat beater attachment, cream the butter with the sugar and ground hazelnuts. Gradually incorporate the eggs, then refrigerate for 30 minutes.

FOR THE RHUBARB JELLY

In a saucepan, bring the rhubarb juice to a boil. Combine the sugar, agar, and xanthan gum and add to the juice. Incorporate using an immersion (stick) blender, then refrigerate until set. Blend again before use.

FOR THE CANDIED RHUBARB

Peel the rhubarb and cut off the ends. Put into a vacuum bag and seal at 100-percent vacuum. Cook sous vide in a steam oven (or water bath) at 145°F (63°C) for 2 hours. When cool, remove the candied rhubarb from the bag and chop into small pieces.

FOR ASSEMBLY

Preheat the oven to 340°F (170°C/Gas Mark 3½). Fill the shortbread tart shells (cases) with hazelnut cream and add one-half of the small pieces of candied rhubarb. Set aside the remainder for finishing. Bake for 8 minutes, let cool for about 15 minutes, then fill to the top with rhubarb jelly. Refrigerate for about 30 minutes. Make a tasteful arrangement of candied rhubarb stalks of different sizes to re-create the shape of a calisson candy.

For the vanilla ganache

See page 340

For the reconstituted speculoos
shortbread

½ quantity (500 g) speculoos
shortbread dough

⅔ cup (150 g) cocoa butter

For the vanilla praline

1 cup (150 g) whole almonds

1 vanilla bean (pod)

½ cup (100 g) superfine (caster)
sugar

For the vanilla sponge cake
●

1 cup (100 g) ground almonds

⅓ cup plus 1 tablespoon (90 g)
packed brown sugar

⅓ cup (40 g) all-purpose (plain)
flour

1 teaspoon (4 g) baking powder

scant 1 teaspoon (5 g) salt

3⅔ extra-large (UK large/135 g)
egg whites (½ cup)

2 extra-large (UK large/40 g) egg
yolks (2½ tablespoons)

5 teaspoons (25 g) whipping cream

For the speculoos shortbread
●

⅞ cup (1¾ sticks/200 g) unsalted
butter, softened

1 cup (200 g) packed dark vergeoise
sugar or dark brown sugar

⅓ cup (60 g) superfine (caster)
sugar

scant ½ teaspoon (2 g) salt

1½ tablespoons (10 g) ground cinnamon

1 small (40 g) egg

2 tablespoons (15 g) milk

3¼ cups (400 g) all-purpose (plain)
flour, sifted

2¼ teaspoons (10 g) baking powder

1¼ teaspoons (6 g) vanilla paste

3 tablespoons (40 g) unsalted
butter, melted

1½ tablespoons (20 g) superfine sugar

For the caramel sauce

See page 335

For the white chocolate coating

See page 338

23

FOR THE VANILLA GANACHE

Make a vanilla ganache as described on page 340.

FOR THE VANILLA PRALINE

Preheat the oven to 330°F (165°C/Gas Mark 3). Roast the almonds and vanilla bean in the oven for 15 minutes. Heat the sugar and 6 tablespoons (70 g water) to 230°F (110°C). Add the almonds and vanilla bean (pod), stir to coat well in the syrup, and let caramelize. Let the caramel cool completely, then remove the vanilla bean before processing to a paste.

FOR THE SPECULOOS SHORTBREAD

Preheat the oven to 340°F (170°C/Gas Mark 3½). Mix the butter with the vergeoise sugar, superfine sugar, salt, and cinnamon. Gradually incorporate the egg. Add the milk and finish with the sifted flour and baking powder. On a baking sheet lined with a Silpat baking mat, roll out the shortbread to an ⅛-inch (4-mm) thickness. Bake for about 10 minutes. Keep the oven at 340°F (170°C/Gas Mark 3½).

FOR THE RECONSTITUTED SPECULOOS SHORTBREAD

Mix the shortbread dough with the melted cocoa butter. Roll out the dough to an ⅛-inch (3-mm) thickness and cut out an 8-inch (20-cm)-diameter disk. Place the disk inside a 6¼-inch (16-cm)-diameter pastry ring on a baking sheet lined with a Silpat mat. Bake at 340°F (170°C/Gas Mark 3½) for about 10 minutes. Let cool.

FOR THE VANILLA SPONGE CAKE

Preheat the oven to 330°F (165°C/Gas Mark 3). Mix the ground almonds, brown sugar, flour, baking powder, and salt with 2½ tablespoons (25 g) of the egg whites, the egg yolks, cream, and vanilla paste. Add the melted butter. In an electric stand mixer with a whisk attachment, beat the remaining egg whites, then add the superfine sugar and beat until stiff. Incorporate the beaten egg whites into the batter. Put a 6¼-inch (16-cm)-diameter pastry ring onto a baking sheet lined with a Silpat mat and pipe in the batter. Bake at 350°F (175°C/Gas Mark 4) for 8 minutes, turning the sheet around halfway through.

FOR THE CARAMEL SAUCE

Make the caramel sauce as described on page 335.

FOR THE WHITE CHOCOLATE COATING

Make the white chocolate coating as described on page 338.

FOR ASSEMBLY

Whip the ganache with a hand mixer. Carefully lift off the ring from the speculoos tart shell (case). Replace it with another pastry ring of the same size lined with an acetate strip. Spread a layer of vanilla praline over the shell and place the sponge over it. Pour it over the caramel and freeze for about 2 hours. Pipe the ganache over the entire surface of a 7-inch (18-cm)-diameter Pavoni silicone entremets mold. Pipe more in the middle so the insert is well centered. Add the insert and cover with ganache. Smooth with a spatula (palette knife). Freeze for about 6 hours, until set. Carefully unmold.

FOR FINISHING

Use a size 105 Saint-Honoré tip (nozzle) to pipe the ganache petals. Start by piping a tight ring in the center of the cake to form the heart of a rose. Then pipe semicircular petals all around it, gradually increasing them in size, until the entire cake is covered. Use a spray gun to uniformly flock the cake with white chocolate coating.

NATURTiUM

For the honey ganache

1½ tablespoons (10 g) peeled and grated fresh ginger

1 cup (240 g) whipping cream

5¼ extra-large (UK large/100 g) egg yolks (3 tablespoons)

3 tablespoons (60 g) propolis honey

3¾ teaspoons (21 g) gelatin mass (1 teaspoon/3 g gelatin powder hydrated in 3¾ teaspoons/18 g water)

1¾ cups (400 g) mascarpone cheese

For the lime gel

3 limes

2½ teaspoons (10 g) olive oil

3 tablespoons plus 2 teaspoons (75 g) golden (runny) honey

2 tablespoons plus 1 teaspoon (30 g) glucose

½ cup (15 g) fresh sage

⅓ cup (15 g) fresh mint

¼ cup plus 1 tablespoon (15 g) fresh tarragon

½ cup (15 g) food-safe marigold flowers

For the sweet tart shell

See page 342

For the almond and lemon cream

4½ tablespoons (65 g) unsalted butter, softened

⅓ cup (65 g) superfine (caster) sugar

⅔ cup (65 g) ground almonds

¼ cup (25 g) lemon zest

1½ medium (UK small/65 g) eggs (¼ cup plus 1 teaspoon)

For the lemon paste

2 lemons

For the orange chocolate coating

See page 338

For the yellow chocolate coating

See page 338

For finishing

Food-safe nasturtium flowers

FOR THE HONEY GANACHE

Combine the ginger and cream in a saucepan and bring to a boil. Beat the yolks with the propolis honey. Pour a little boiling cream over this mixture, then return it to the saucepan to make a crème anglaise. Cook for 2 minutes, then incorporate the gelatin mass using an immersion (stick) blender. Filter through a conical sieve and add the mascarpone. Refrigerate for about 12 hours.

FOR THE LIME GEL

Wash the limes, slice off the ends, and cut into pieces, then transfer to a blender and process to a paste. In a saucepan, combine the lemon paste with the olive oil, golden honey, and glucose and bring to a boil until smooth. Incorporate the marigolds using an immersion stick blender.

FOR THE SWEET TART SHELL

Make the sweet tart shell (case) as described on page 342.

FOR THE ALMOND AND LEMON CREAM

In a stand mixer fitted with a flat beater attachment, cream the butter with the sugar, ground almonds, and lemon zest. Incorporate the eggs.

FOR THE LEMON PASTE

Wash the lemons. Poach the whole lemons in a saucepan of boiling water for about 20 minutes. Transfer to a blender and process to a paste.

FOR THE ORANGE AND YELLOW CHOCOLATE COATINGS

Make the orange chocolate coating, followed by the yellow chocolate coating, as described on page 338.

FOR ASSEMBLY

Fill the tart shell with the almond and lemon cream. Bake for 8 minutes. Let cool for 15 minutes. Spread a thin layer of lemon paste over the cream and fill to the top with lemon gel. Smooth with a spatula (palette knife), then make a lemon gel dome in the center. Freeze.

FOR FINISHING

Whip the ganache with a hand mixer. Use a size 125 Saint-Honoré tip (nozzle) to pipe flowers on a Silpat mat. Pipe three semicircles to form the petals of each flower. Freeze the flowers for 4 hours, then use a spray gun to flock three-quarters of them with the orange chocolate coating and the remaining one-quarter with the yellow chocolate coating. Arrange the flowers on the cake. For the pistils, use a pastry (piping) bag fitted with a $1/16$-inch (2-mm) plain tip to pipe lines of ganache. Decorate everything with the nasturtium flowers. Refrigerate for 4 hours.

BABA

For the baba batter

See page 341

For the rum cream

7/8 cup (200 g) whipping cream

1½ tablespoons (20 g) superfine (caster) sugar

1 vanilla bean (pod)

4 teaspoons (20 g) Havana Club Selección de Maestros rum

For the baba soaking syrup

See page 343

For the Chantilly cream

2¼ cups (520 g) whipping cream

2 vanilla beans (pods)

1½ tablespoons (20 g) superfine (caster) sugar

3½ tablespoons (50 g) mascarpone cheese

2½ teaspoons (14 g) gelatin mass (½ teaspoon/2 g gelatin powder hydrated in 2½ teaspoons/12 g water)

For the vanilla glaze

⅓ cup (100 g) neutral glaze

½ teaspoon (1 g) vanilla pearls (or vanilla seeds)

FOR THE BABA BATTER

Make the baba batter as described on page 341.

Preheat the oven to 350°F (175°C/Gas Mark 4). Pipe the batter into a 7-inch (18-cm)-diameter brioche mold. Bake at 350°F (180°C/Gas Mark 4) for 15 minutes, then at 325°F (160°C/Gas Mark 3) for 15 minutes and finally at 275°F (140°C/Gas Mark 1) for 6 minutes.

FOR THE RUM CREAM

In a saucepan, heat the cream combined with the sugar and the split and scraped vanilla bean and seeds. Remove from the heat, cover, and let infuse for 10 minutes. Filter through a conical sieve, add the rum, and refrigerate.

FOR THE BABA SOAKING SYRUP

Make the baba soaking syrup as described on page 343.

FOR THE CHANTILLY CREAM

In a saucepan, combine one-third of the cream with the split and scraped vanilla beans and seeds and the sugar, then bring to a boil. Pour the boiling mixture over the mascarpone and gelatin mass. Filter through a conical sieve and blend. Gradually incorporate the remaining cream. Refrigerate.

FOR ASSEMBLY

The day before, in a saucepan heat the syrup to 145°F (62°C), then completely immerse the baba. Let stand for about 12 hours. The next day, use a spoon to hollow out the center of the baba. Pipe part of the rum cream inside.

FOR FINISHING

Use a hand mixer to whip the remaining rum cream. In a stand mixer fitted with a whisk attachment, whip the Chantilly cream. Use a pastry (piping) bag fitted with a size 14 tip (nozzle) to pipe balls of whipped cream petals over the baba, pressing to form a ball on the outside edge and extending the petal toward the center. Finish by forming the center of the baba flower from a large ball of rum cream.

FOR THE VANILLA GLAZE

In a saucepan, combine the neutral glaze with the vanilla pearls and bring to a boil. Transfer the mixture to a spray gun and flock the cake with glaze.

DAISY

For the coconut ganache

1 cup (240 g) whipping cream

⅔ cup (50 g) shredded coconut, toasted

6 large (UK medium/100 g) egg yolks (⅜ cup)

¼ cup (50 g) superfine (caster) sugar

4 teaspoons (21 g) gelatin mass (1 teaspoon/3 g gelatin powder hydrated in 4 teaspoons/18 g water)

2⅔ cups (650 g) coconut puree

1¾ cups (400 g) mascarpone cheese

For the diamond shortbread tart shell

See page 342

For the coconut praline

See page 342

For the coconut crisp

See page 337

For the coconut gel

1 cup (250 g) coconut puree

1 teaspoon (2.5 g) xanthan gum

For the lemon gel

2½ cups (600 g) lemon juice

⅓ cup (60 g) superfine (caster) sugar

1½ tablespoons (12 g) agar powder

For the almond and coconut dacquoise

3¾ large (UK medium/125 g) egg whites (½ cup)

¼ cup (55 g) superfine (caster) sugar

½ cup plus 1 tablespoon (55 g) ground almonds

⅔ cup (55 g) shredded coconut

2 tablespoons plus 2 teaspoons (20 g) all-purpose (plain) flour

⅔ cup (85 g) confectioners' (icing) sugar

For the white chocolate coating

See page 338

For the yellow chocolate coating

See page 338

For the orange chocolate coating

See page 338

FOR THE COCONUT GANACHE

Combine the cream with the toasted coconut in a saucepan and bring to a boil. Beat the yolks with the superfine sugar. Pour a little of the boiling cream over this mixture, then return it to the saucepan to make a crème anglaise. Cook for 2 minutes, then incorporate the gelatin mass and coconut puree using an immersion (stick) blender. Filter through a conical sieve and add the mascarpone. Refrigerate for about 12 hours.

FOR THE DIAMOND SHORTBREAD TART SHELL

Make the tart shell (case) as described on page 342.

FOR THE COCONUT PRALINE AND THE COCONUT CRISP

Make the hazelnut praline as described on page 342. Make the coconut crisp as described on page 337.

FOR THE COCONUT GEL

Mix the coconut puree with the xanthan gum.

FOR THE LEMON GEL

In a saucepan, bring the lemon juice to a boil. Add the superfine sugar and agar powder and incorporate using an immersion blender. Refrigerate until set.

FOR THE ALMOND AND COCONUT DACQUOISE

Preheat the oven to 340°F (170°C/Gas Mark 3½). Make a French meringue by beating the egg whites until stiff, incorporating the superfine sugar in three batches. The meringue is ready when it forms a peak on the end of the whisk without collapsing. Fold in the dry ingredients. Pipe the dacquoise batter into a 9½-inch (24-cm)-diameter pastry ring. Bake for about 18 minutes. Let cool on a rack.

FOR THE WHITE, YELLOW, AND ORANGE CHOCOLATE COATINGS

Make the three different coatings as described on page 338.

FOR ASSEMBLY AND FINISHING

Whip the ganache in a stand mixer. Make the insert: Place the dacquoise inside a 9½-inch (24-cm)-diameter pastry ring. Spread with a layer of coconut gel. Pipe over with dots of coconut praline and lemon gel at a ratio of four praline dots to each lemon gel dot. Freeze for about 3 hours. Pipe ganache over the entire surface of a 10¼-inch (26-cm)-diameter entremets mold. Pipe more in the middle so the insert will be well centered. Add the insert and cover with ganache. Smooth with a spatula (palette knife). Freeze for about 6 hours, until set. Carefully unmold. Spread a layer of coconut crisp over the tart shell, followed by a thin layer of lemon gel. Introduce the frozen insert.

Step 1
On a Silpat or a small metal stand, use a pastry (piping) bag fitted with size 104 Saint-Honoré tip (nozzle) to pipe ganache daisies. Start by piping a small upright line. When you reach the end, form a semicircle the size of the tip of your index finger and return to the starting point. Repeat the process, petal by petal, to form a daisy. Make about 20 daisies in total to cover the cake. Let set in the freezer for about 4 hours. Use a spray gun to uniformly cover the petals with the white chocolate coating.

Step 2
For the daisy hearts, use silicone molds to make soft, 1¼-inch (3-cm)-diameter disks of lemon gel. Let set in the freezer for about 3 hours. Use a spray gun to uniformly cover the petals with the yellow chocolate coating, then flock lightly with orange chocolate coating. Place the flocked hearts in the center of the daisies, then place in an attractive arrangement on the entremets. Refrigerate for about 4 hours before serving.

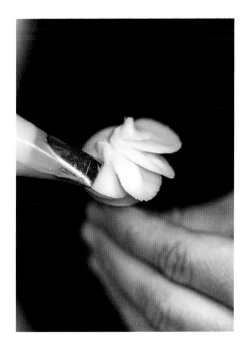

VANiLLA

LEMON

For the vanilla ganache

1 cup (235 g) whipping cream

1 vanilla bean (pod)

1¾ ounces (50 g) ivory white couverture chocolate, chopped

2½ teaspoons (14 g) gelatin mass (⅜ teaspoon/2 g gelatin powder hydrated in 2½ teaspoons/12 g water)

For the sweet tart shell

See page 342

For the almond and vanilla cream

See page 336

For the lemon marmalade

1 vanilla bean (pod)

1 (115 g) lemon

½ cup (115 g) lemon juice

1 tablespoon (25 g) golden (runny) honey

For the lemon crémeux

¼ cup (70 g) lemon juice

2 small (80 g) eggs (⅓ cup)

1 teaspoon (7 g) golden (runny) honey

1¼ teaspoons (7 g) gelatin mass (⅜ teaspoon/1 g gelatin powder hydrated in 1¼ teaspoons/6 g water)

6 tablespoons (85 g) unsalted butter

For the yellow chocolate coating

See page 338

For the gold glitter

7/8 cup (220 g) kirsch

1½ cups (120 g) gold luster dust

For assembly

10 lemon suprêmes

FOR THE VANILLA GANACHE

The previous day, heat half the cream in a saucepan. Add the split and scraped vanilla bean (pod) and seeds. Remove from the heat, cover, and let infuse for about 10 minutes. Heat the mixture again and filter through a conical sieve. Pour it over the chopped chocolate and gelatin mass, then add the remaining cream. Blend to a smooth ganache. Refrigerate for about 12 hours.

FOR THE SWEET TART SHELL

Make the tart shell (case) as described on page 342.

FOR THE ALMOND AND VANILLA CREAM

Make the almond and vanilla cream as described on page 336.

FOR THE LEMON MARMALADE

Split the vanilla bean and scrape out the seeds. Wash the lemons, cut off and discard the ends, cut into pieces, and process in a blender with the vanilla seeds. In a saucepan, combine all the ingredients and bring to a boil. Let cool.

FOR THE LEMON CRÉMEUX

In a saucepan, bring the lemon juice to a boil. Add the eggs and honey. Heat to 220°F (105°C), stirring constantly. Remove from the heat and incorporate the gelatin mass and butter.

FOR THE YELLOW CHOCOLATE COATING

Make the yellow chocolate coating as described on page 338.

FOR THE GOLD GLITTER

Mix the kirsch with the gold luster dust.

FOR ASSEMBLY

Preheat the oven to 340°F (170°C/Gas Mark 3½). Fill the tart shell with almond and vanilla cream. Bake for 8 minutes. Let cool for about 15 minutes, then fill halfway with marmalade. Cut up the lemon sections and arrange a few pieces on top, pressing lightly. Cover everything with lemon crémeux. Smooth with a spatula (palette knife).

FOR FINISHING

Whip the ganache with a hand mixer. Using a metal stand and a size 20 Saint-Honoré tip (nozzle), pipe ganache flames over the tart, starting from the outside and working your way toward the center. Make an outer ring of flames and continue in a staggered pattern. Use a spray gun to uniformly flock the tart with yellow chocolate coating. Repeat the process with the gold glitter. Refrigerate for about 4 hours before serving.

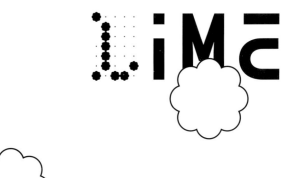

For the sweet tart shell

See page 342

For the almond and lime cream

4½ tablespoons (65 g) unsalted butter, softened

⅓ cup (65 g) superfine (caster) sugar

⅔ cup (65 g) ground almonds

¼ cup (25 g) lime zest

1½ medium (UK small/65 g) eggs (¼ cup)

For the lime gel

3 limes

2½ teaspoons (10 g) olive oil

¼ cup (75 g) golden (runny) honey

2 tablespoons (30 g) glucose powder

½ cup (15 g) fresh sage

⅓ cup (15 g) fresh mint

¼ cup (15 g) fresh tarragon

½ cup (15 g) food-safe pot marigold (calendula) flowers

For the lime crémeux

¼ cup plus 1 tablespoon (70 g) lime juice

2 small (80 g) eggs (⅓ cup)

1 teaspoon (7 g) golden (runny) honey

1¼ teaspoons (7 g) gelatin mass (⅜ teaspoon/1 g gelatin powder hydrated in 1¼ teaspoons/6 g water)

6 tablespoons (85 g) unsalted butter

For the meringue

See page 341

For finishing

Non-melting snow white topping sugar, such as Codineige or King Arthur (optional)

FOR THE SWEET TART SHELL

Make the tart shell (case) as described on page 342.

FOR THE ALMOND AND LIME CREAM

In a stand mixer fitted with a flat beater attachment, cream the butter with the sugar, ground almonds, and zest. Gradually incorporate the eggs, then refrigerate for about 30 minutes.

FOR THE LIME GEL

Wash the limes, cut off and discard the ends, cut into pieces, and process in a blender to form a paste. In a saucepan, combine the lime paste with the olive oil, honey, and glucose until smooth. Incorporate the sage, mint, tarragon, and flowers using an immersion (stick) blender.

FOR THE LIME CRÉMEUX

In a saucepan, bring the lemon juice to a boil. Add the eggs and honey. Heat to 220°F (105°C), stirring constantly. Remove from the heat and incorporate the gelatin mass and butter.

FOR THE MERINGUE

Make the meringue as described on page 341.

FOR ASSEMBLY

Preheat the oven to 340°F (170°C/Gas Mark 3½). Fill the tart shell with almond and lime cream and bake for 8 minutes. Let cool for about 15 minutes, then fill to the top with lemon crémeux. Smooth with a spatula (palette knife). Place in the freezer until the crémeux is frozen.

FOR FINISHING

Use a pastry (piping) bag fitted with a plain tip (nozzle) to pipe the meringue into rings of ball-like petals. After piping a ball, make a short upward, then downward stroke, as if breaking off but without prolonging the movement. Pipe the following ball next to the first and continue in this way around the cake. Repeat the process two or three times to make rings with increasingly reduced diameters. When starting a new ring, always stagger the placement of the first petal. Sprinkle lightly all over with the snow sugar (if using). Bake at 325°F (165°C/Gas Mark 3) for 16 minutes, then take out and let cool. Finish by making a center of lime gel.

ViOLT

For the black currant and violet ganache

⅝ cup (140 g) whipping cream

3 extra-large (UK large/60 g) egg yolks (¼ cup)

2½ tablespoons (30 g) superfine (caster) sugar

2½ teaspoons (14 g) gelatin mass (⅝ teaspoon/2 g gelatin powder hydrated in 2½ teaspoons/12 g water)

⅞ cup (230 g) black currant puree

1 cup (230 g) mascarpone cheese

Natural violet essence

For the black currant gel

●

2 cups (500 g) black currant juice

¼ cup (50 g) superfine (caster) sugar

1 tablespoon (8 g) agar powder

1 teaspoon (3 g) xanthan gum

4½ cups (500 g) black currants

For the white chocolate coating

●

See page 338

For Finishing

●

1⅓ cups (150 g) black currants

For the purple chocolate coating

●

½ cup (100 g) cocoa butter

3½ ounces (100 g) white chocolate

¼ teaspoon (1 g) purple food coloring powder

For the black currant glaze

●

¾ cup (250 g) neutral glaze

2½ tablespoons (40 g) black currant puree

2½ teaspoons (10 g) olive oil

FOR THE BLACK CURRANT AND VIOLET GANACHE

In a saucepan, bring the cream to a boil. Beat the yolks with the sugar. Pour a little boiling cream over this mixture, then return it to the saucepan to make a crème anglaise. Cook for 2 minutes, then incorporate the gelatin mass and black currant puree using an immersion (stick) blender. Filter through a conical sieve and add the mascarpone and a few drops of violet essence. Refrigerate for about 12 hours.

FOR THE BLACK CURRANT GEL

In a saucepan, bring the black currant juice to a boil. Add the sugar, agar, and xanthan gum, blend with an immersion (stick) blender, then refrigerate to set. Blend again, set aside a small amount of the gel, and add the black currants, halved, to the rest of the gel. Pour into 3¼-inch (8-cm)-long oval (calisson-shaped) silicone molds. Place in the freezer 1 hour to make the inserts.

FOR THE WHITE CHOCOLATE COATING

Make the white chocolate coating as described on page 338.

Dip the frozen inserts into the coating at 95°F (35°C) and drain off the excess.

FOR THE PURPLE CHOCOLATE COATING

Melt the cocoa butter and pour it over the chopped chocolate. Add the food coloring and blend with an immersion blender until smooth.

FOR THE BLACK CURRANT GLAZE

In a saucepan, combine all the ingredients, bring to a boil, and mix well.

FOR FINISHING

Cover the inserts with the black currant gel. Use a pastry (piping) bag fitted with a ½-inch (12-mm) plain tip (nozzle) to pipe irregularly shaped ganache petals all around each coated insert, working from the top down. The idea is to attach the petals to the gel and give volume to the edges. Use a spray gun to uniformly flock the dessert with the purple chocolate coating. Glaze the black currants and arrange them over the top. Refrigerate for about 4 hours before serving.

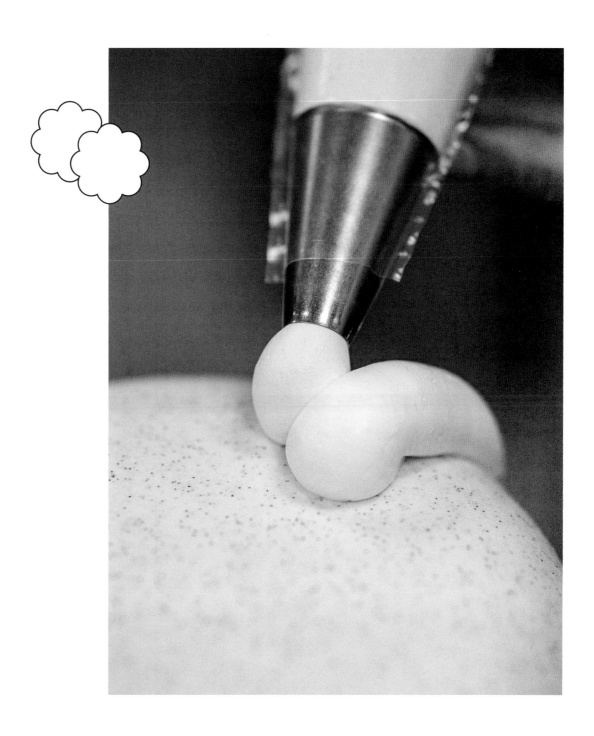

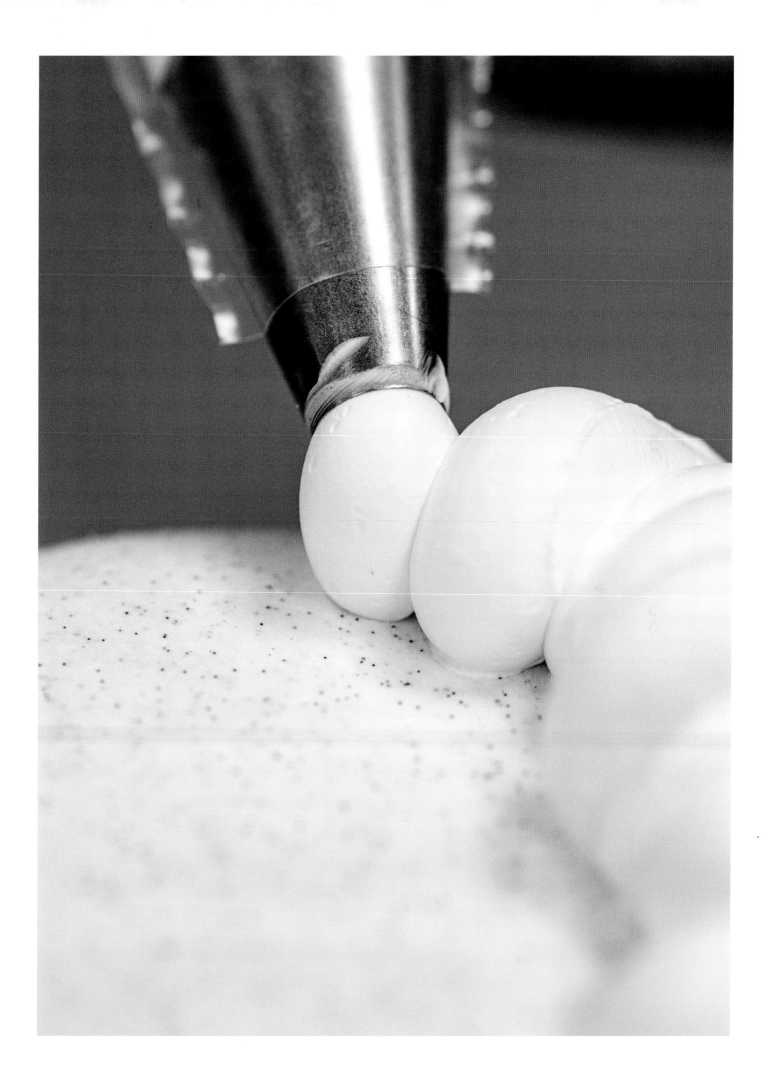

HONEY

For the honey ganache

1 cup (240 g) whipping cream

6 large (UK extra-large/100 g) egg yolks (⅜ cup)

3 tablespoons (60 g) honey

3¾ teaspoons (21 g) gelatin mass (1 teaspoon/3 g gelatin powder hydrated in 3¾ teaspoons/18 g water)

1¾ cups (400 g) mascarpone cheese

For the almond and honey praline

See page 342

For the almond and honey crisp

See page 336

For the almond and honey dacquoise

6 large (UK medium/180 g) egg whites (¾ cup)

¼ cup (75 g) honeydew (forest) honey

1⅔ cups (160 g) ground almonds

1¼ cups (160 g) confectioners' (icing) sugar

For the lemon and honey gel

¼ cup (50 g) superfine (caster) sugar

1 tablespoon (8 g) agar powder

2 cups (500 g) lemon juice

¾ teaspoon (2 g) xanthan gum

2¼ teaspoons (15 g) lavender honey

⅓ cup (70 g) lemon suprêmes

For the pollen gel

2 cups (500 g) lemon juice

¼ cup (50 g) superfine (caster) sugar

1¾ teaspoons (5 g) agar powder

2½ tablespoons (25 g) bee pollen

For the yellow chocolate coating

See page 338

For the orange chocolate coating

See page 338

For finishing

2½ tablespoons (25 g) bee pollen

FOR THE HONEY GANACHE

In a saucepan, bring the cream to a boil. Beat the yolks with the honey. Pour a little boiling cream over this mixture, then return it to the saucepan to make a crème anglaise. Cook for 2 minutes, then incorporate the gelatin mass using an immersion (stick) blender. Filter through a conical sieve and add the mascarpone. Refrigerate for about 12 hours.

FOR THE ALMOND AND HONEY PRALINE

Make the almond and honey praline as described on page 342.

FOR THE ALMOND AND HONEY CRISP

Make the almond and honey crisp as described on page 336.

FOR THE ALMOND AND HONEY DACQUOISE

Preheat the oven to 340°F (170°C/Gas Mark 3½). In a stand mixer fitted with a whisk attachment, beat the egg whites until stiff. In a saucepan, bring the honey to a boil. Using a silicone spatula, fold the honey into the beaten egg whites, being careful to avoid letting the mixture collapse. Sift the ground almonds with the confectioners' sugar and fold into the mixture. Pipe a ⅜-inch (1-cm)-thick layer of dacquoise batter inside a 9½-inch (24-cm)-diameter pastry ring. Bake for 16 minutes.

FOR THE LEMON AND HONEY GEL

Mix together the superfine sugar and agar powder. In a saucepan, bring the lemon juice to a boil, then add the superfine sugar and agar mixture. Let cool, then use an immersion (stick) blender to loosen it well, then incorporate the xanthan gum, followed by the honey. Cut the lemon sections into small and irregular pieces, then incorporate them into the gel.

FOR THE POLLEN GEL

Mix together the superfine sugar and agar powder. In a saucepan, bring the lemon juice to a boil. Add the superfine sugar and agar mixture and incorporate using an immersion blender. Let cool, then incorporate the pollen.

FOR THE YELLOW AND ORANGE CHOCOLATE COATINGS

Make the yellow chocolate coating, followed by the orange chocolate coating, as described on page 338.

FOR ASSEMBLY

Whip the ganache in a stand mixer. Make the insert: Carefully lift off the ring from the dacquoise, line it with an acetate strip, and cover with an even layer, about $\frac{1}{16}$ inch (2 mm) thick, of the almond and honey crisp. Insert the dacquoise disk. Finally, pipe dots of lemon and honey gel and pollen gel over the entire surface of the disk. The total thickness of the insert should not exceed 1 inch (2.5 cm). Freeze for about 6 hours. Pipe ganache over the entire surface of a 7-inch (18-cm)-diameter Pavoni silicone entremets mold. Pipe more in the middle to help center the insert. Add the insert and cover with ganache. Smooth with a spatula (palette knife). Let set in the freezer for about 6 hours. Carefully unmold.

FOR FINISHING

Use a size 104 Saint-Honoré tip (nozzle) to pipe large ganache petals separately on parchment (baking) paper. To make the petals, start by piping a straight line. When you reach the end, form a semicircle the size of the tip of your index finger and return to the starting point. The petals should touch to form a flower, leaving a 1½-inch (4-cm)-diameter circular hollow. Use a spray gun to cover the petals uniformly with yellow chocolate coating, then create an ombré effect by spraying the tips with orange chocolate coating. Arrange the petals on the cake. Make the heart of the flower by filling the hollow in the center with fresh pollen. Refrigerate for about 4 hours before serving.

CAMELLIA

For the tea ganache

3¼ cups (780 g) whipping cream

⅔ cup (50 g) white tea

6¼ ounces (175 g) white couverture chocolate, chopped

2½ tablespoons (42 g) gelatin mass (2 teaspoons/7 g gelatin powder hydrated in 2½ tablespoons/35 g water)

For the camellia gel

1⅛ cups (275 g) lemon juice

3 tablespoons plus 1 teaspoon (15 g) white tea

1½ tablespoons (20 g) superfine (caster) sugar

1 teaspoon (3 g) agar powder

⅜ teaspoon (1 g) xanthan gum

⅓ cup plus 1½ tablespoons (100 g) aloe vera gel

For the almond and green cardamom crisp

3½ cups (500 g) unblanched almonds

⅔ cup (130 g) superfine (caster) sugar

¼ cup (50 g) cocoa butter

2 cups (100 g) feuilletine flakes

¼ cup (25 g) green cardamom pods, crushed to remove the seeds

½ teaspoon (2 g) fleur de sel

For the white chocolate coating

See page 338

For the almond and lemon dacquoise

3 lemons

2½ large (UK medium/80 g) egg whites (⅓ cup)

3 tablespoons (35 g) superfine (caster) sugar

¾ cup (70 g) ground almonds

2 tablespoons (15 g) all-purpose (plain) flour

⅓ cup plus 2 tablespoons (55 g) confectioners' (icing) sugar

For finishing

Non-melting snow white topping sugar, such as Codineige or King Arthur

FOR THE TEA GANACHE

The previous day, heat half the cream in a saucepan. Add the tea. Remove from the heat, cover, and let infuse for about 10 minutes. Heat the mixture again and filter through a conical sieve. Pour it over the chopped chocolate and gelatin mass, then add the remaining cream. Mix to make a smooth ganache. Refrigerate for about 12 hours.

FOR THE ALMOND AND GREEN CARDAMOM CRISP

Dry the almonds in the oven at 212°F (100°C) for 1 hour. In a saucepan, heat 2½ tablespoons (40 g) water with the superfine sugar to 230°F (110°C). Add the dried almonds and coat well with the syrup. Let cool, then use an immersion (stick) blender to crush and blend the almonds with the melted cocoa butter, feuilletine flakes, cardamom seeds, and fleur de sel.

FOR THE ALMOND AND LEMON DACQUOISE

Preheat the oven to 340°F (170°C/Gas Mark 3½). Use a Microplane grater to grate the zest from the lemons. Make a meringue by beating the egg whites until stiff, then incorporating the superfine sugar in three batches. The meringue is ready when it forms a peak on the end of the whisk without collapsing. With a silicone spatula, fold in the ground almonds, flour, confectioners' sugar, and zest. Pipe the dacquoise batter into a 6¼-inch (16-cm)-diameter pastry ring. Bake for 16 minutes.

FOR THE CAMELLIA GEL

In a saucepan, bring the lemon juice to a boil. Add the tea and let boil for 5 minutes. Add the superfine sugar, agar, and xanthan gum. Incorporate using an immersion (stick) blender and refrigerate until set. Then blend again. Mix with the aloe vera and cut into cubes.

FOR THE WHITE CHOCOLATE COATING

Make the white chocolate coating as described on page 338.

FOR ASSEMBLY

Whip the ganache with a hand mixer. Spread a layer of the crisp inside a 6¼-inch (16-cm)-diameter pastry ring. Insert the dacquoise disk. Spread a layer of gel over the top. Freeze for about 6 hours. Pipe ganache over the entire surface of a 7-inch (18-cm)-diameter Pavoni silicone entremets mold. Pipe more in the middle to help center the insert. Add the insert and cover with ganache. Smooth with a spatula (palette knife). Let set in the freezer for about 6 hours. Carefully unmold.

FOR FINISHING

Use a pastry (piping) bag fitted with a size 125 Saint-Honoré tip (nozzle) to pipe the ganache petals, starting at the bottom of the cake and piping toward the top. Hold the pastry bag horizontally and form large petals. Use a spray gun to uniformly flock the entremets with the white chocolate coating. Dust the flower with a fine covering of snow sugar through a fine-mesh sieve. Refrigerate for about 4 hours before serving.

GRAPEFRUIT

For the sansho ganache

2¼ cups (530 g) whipping cream

½ cup (120 g) milk

2¾ teaspoons (3 g) fresh sansho berries

5 ounces (145 g) white couverture chocolate, chopped

1½ tablespoons (25 g) gelatin mass (1 teaspoon/3.5 g gelatin powder hydrated in 1½ tablespoons/21.5 g water)

For the joconde cake

See page 335

For the grapefruit and sansho marmalade insert

3¾ teaspoons (15 g) superfine (caster) sugar

1 teaspoon (2.5 g) agar powder

⅔ cup (150 g) lemon juice

⅜ teaspoon (1 g) xanthan gum

⅓ cup (75 g) candied grapefruit

¼ cup (25 g) grapefruit zest

⅓ cup (75 g) fresh grapefruit

scant ¼ teaspoon (1 g) sansho powder

1 teaspoon (1 g) fresh sansho berries

For the lemon gel

2½ tablespoons (10 g) superfine (caster) sugar

¾ teaspoon (2 g) agar powder

⅓ cup plus 1 tablespoon (100 g) lemon juice

For the pink salt

1 quantity (100 g) lemon gel (see above)

2¾ cups (50 g) dried rose petals

For the yellow chocolate coating

See page 338

For the pink chocolate coating

See page 338

For finishing

1 grapefruit

61

FOR THE SANSHO GANACHE

The previous day, heat half the cream and the milk in a saucepan with the sansho berries. Pour it over the chopped chocolate and gelatin mass, then add the remaining cream. Blend to a smooth ganache and filter through a conical sieve. Refrigerate for about 12 hours.

FOR THE JOCONDE CAKE

Make the joconde cake as described on page 335.

FOR THE GRAPEFRUIT AND SANSHO MARMALADE INSERT

Mix together the sugar and agar powder. In a saucepan, bring the lemon juice to a boil, then add the sugar and agar mixture. Let cool, then use an immersion (stick) blender to loosen it well, then incorporate the xanthan gum. Cut the three types of grapefruit into cubes and add to the gel along with the sansho powder and berries. Pour the marmalade into a 6¼-inch (16-cm)-diameter and ⅜-inch (1-cm)-deep mold. Freeze for about 4 hours, until set.

FOR THE LEMON GEL

Combine the sugar and agar powder. In a saucepan, bring the lemon juice to a boil, then add the sugar and agar mixture. Incorporate using an immersion (stick) blender and refrigerate until set.

FOR THE PINK GEL

Blend the lemon gel with the petals.

FOR THE YELLOW CHOCOLATE COATING

Make the yellow chocolate coating as described on page 338.

FOR THE PINK CHOCOLATE COATING

Make the pink chocolate coating as described on page 338.

FOR ASSEMBLY

Whip the ganache with a hand mixer. Place the joconde disk inside a 6¼-inch (16-cm)-diameter pastry ring lined with an acetate strip. Cover the inside with a thin layer of ganache. Introduce the frozen insert. Cover with a layer of gel and smooth with a spatula (palette knife). Freeze for about 6 hours. Pipe ganache over the entire surface of a 7-inch (18-cm)-diameter Pavoni silicone entremets mold. Pipe more in the middle to help center the insert. Introduce the insert, cover with ganache, and smooth with a spatula (palette knife). Freeze for about 6 hours, until set, before carefully unmolding.

FOR FiNiSHiNG

Step 1
Use a pastry (piping) bag fitted with a size 125 Saint-Honoré tip (nozzle) to pipe whipped semicircular ganache rose petals around the outside of the entremets.

Step 2
Use a size 104 Saint-Honoré tip to pipe ribbons of ganache on the inside without any particular direction, as if the ganache has "come to life."

Step 3
In the center, use a size 4 plain tip to pipe a ring of flower pistils in ganache.

Use a spray gun to uniformly flock three-quarters of the entremets with yellow chocolate coating. Then flock the lowest quarter in pink chocolate coating. Peel the grapefruit and separate the sections. Microwave for 15-30 seconds. Make a cut into the pith at the top of each section and open the membrane outward to remove the flesh. Arrange the grapefruit suprêmes in the middle of the entremets.

LiLAC

For the choux pastry sponge cake

2 teaspoons (10 g) milk

1¾ tablespoons (25 g) unsalted butter

¼ cup plus 1½ teaspoons (35 g) cake (Italian "00") flour

1 medium (UK small/45 g) egg

2 extra-large (UK large/40 g) egg yolks

1½ extra large (UK large/80 g) egg whites (⅓ cup)

¼ cup (55 g) superfine (caster) sugar

20 fresh blueberries

For the custard ganache

⅞ cup (200 g) whipping cream

5 large (UK medium/85 g) egg yolks

3½ tablespoons (40 g) superfine (caster) sugar

1 tablespoon (17 g) gelatin mass (¾ teaspoon/2.5 g gelatin powder hydrated in 1 tablespoon/14.5 g water)

1⅓ cups plus 1½ tablespoons (330 g) crème fraîche

2 tablespoons plus 1 teaspoon (35 g) lemon juice

1⅓ cups plus 1½ tablespoons (330 g) mascarpone cheese

For the blueberry and lilac gel

1⅔ cups (400 g) blueberry juice

⅓ cup (15 g) food-safe lilac flowers

3½ tablespoons (40 g) superfine (caster) sugar

2¼ teaspoons (6 g) agar powder

¾ teaspoon (2 g) xanthan gum

For the white chocolate coating

See page 338

For assembly

20 fresh blueberries

FOR THE CHOUX PASTRY SPONGE

Preheat the oven to 325°F (165°C/Gas Mark 3). In a saucepan, bring the milk and butter to a boil. Let boil for 1-2 minutes, then add the flour and stir over low heat until the paste pulls away easily from the sides of the pan. Transfer to a stand mixer fitted with a flat beater attachment. Mix to release the steam, then add the eggs and yolks in three batches. Beat the egg whites until stiff, adding the sugar in three batches. The meringue is ready when it forms a peak on the end of the whisk without collapsing. Fold the meringue into the choux paste in three batches until incorporated and smooth. Pipe the batter into an 8-inch (20-cm)-diameter pastry ring. Insert the blueberries into the batter, then bake for 20-25 minutes, opening the oven door halfway through cooking to prevent condensation. Let cool.

FOR THE CUSTARD GANACHE

In a saucepan, bring the cream to a boil. Beat the yolks with the sugar. Pour a little boiling cream over this mixture, then return it to the saucepan to make a crème anglaise. Let cook for 2 minutes, then use an immersion (stick) blender to incorporate the gelatin mass and crème fraîche, previously mixed with the lemon juice. Filter through a conical sieve and add the mascarpone. Refrigerate for about 12 hours.

FOR THE BLUEBERRY AND LILAC GEL

In a saucepan, combine the blueberry juice with the lilac flowers, bring to a boil, then add the sugar, agar, and xanthan gum. Incorporate using an immersion blender and refrigerate until set.

FOR THE WHITE CHOCOLATE COATING

Make the white chocolate coating as described on page 338.

FOR ASSEMBLY

Whip the ganache with a hand mixer. Carefully lift off the ring from the choux pastry sponge. Replace it with another pastry ring of the same size lined with an acetate strip. The strip should be ⅜-¾ inch (1-2 cm) wider than the height of the pastry ring. Spread a layer of gel over the sponge disk, then arrange the whole blueberries on top. Cover with gel to the top of the blueberries, making the gel layer as smooth as possible. Freeze for about 1 hour. Pipe ganache over the entire surface of a 7-inch (18-cm)-diameter Pavoni silicone entremets mold. Pipe more in the middle so the insert will be well centered. Add the insert and cover with ganache. Smooth with a spatula (palette knife). Freeze for about 1 hour, until set.

FOR FINISHING

Place the cake on a turntable. Use a pastry (piping) bag fitted with a size 125 Saint-Honoré tip (nozzle) to pipe the ganache in a single attempt with the turntable in motion. Hold the pastry bag in your hand at a 60-degree angle, and making small wavelike movements with your wrist, start piping around the bottom of the entremets. Gradually work your way toward the top. Use a spray gun to uniformly flock the entremets with white chocolate coating.

TROPÉZIENNE

For the vanilla ganache

1⅓ cups (312 g) whipping cream

1 vanilla bean (pod)

2½ oz (70 g) white couverture chocolate, chopped

3¼ teaspoons (18 g) gelatin mass (¾ teaspoon/2.5 g gelatin powder hydrated in 3¼ teaspoons/15.5 g water)

For the brioche dough

2 cups (250 g) all-purpose (plain) flour

1 teaspoon (6 g) salt

2½ tablespoons (30 g) superfine (caster) sugar

2¼ teaspoons (10 g) baking powder

2 extra-large (UK large/112 g) eggs

2 tablespoons plus 2 teaspoons (38 g) milk

1¾ tablespoons (25 g) unsalted butter

Pearl sugar

For the soaking syrup

¼ orange

¼ lemon

¼ lime

¼ grapefruit

1¼ cups (250 g) superfine (caster) sugar

½ cup (125 g) orange flower water

For the vanilla pastry cream

½ cup (120 g) milk

1½ tablespoons (20 g) whipping cream

1 vanilla bean (pod)

1 small (40 g) egg

3 tablespoons (35 g) superfine (caster) sugar

1½ teaspoons (10 g) custard powder

1 tablespoon (15 g) unsalted butter, softened

2 tablespoons (30 g) mascarpone cheese

For the crème diplomat

See page 336

FOR THE VANILLA GANACHE

The previous day, heat the cream in a saucepan. Add the split and scraped vanilla bean and seeds. Remove from the heat, cover, and let infuse for about 10 minutes. Pour it over the chopped chocolate and gelatin mass. Blend to a smooth ganache and filter through a conical sieve. Refrigerate for about 12 hours.

FOR THE BRIOCHE DOUGH

Preheat the oven to 340°F (170°C/Gas Mark 3½). In a stand mixer fitted with a dough hook, mix the flour, salt, superfine sugar, baking powder, eggs, and milk on speed 1 for 35 minutes. Add the butter and mix on speed 2 for 8 minutes. Rest the dough in the refrigerator for 10 hours. Transfer the dough to a 7-inch (18-cm)-diameter flower-shape baking pan. Proof the dough at 75-77°F (24-25°C) for 2 hours 30 minutes. Lightly press the dough with your fingers. Sprinkle with the pearl sugar. Bake for 12-13 minutes.

FOR THE SOAKING SYRUP

Zest the orange lemon, lime, and grapefruit. In a saucepan, combine the assorted zest, sugar, and orange flower water with 1 cup (250 g) water and heat the syrup to 215°F (103°C), then let cool. Filter the syrup through a conical sieve and brush over the brioche to soak.

FOR THE VANILLA PASTRY CREAM

Make the vanilla pastry cream as described on page 336.

FOR THE CRÈME DIPLOMAT

Make the crème diplomat as described on page 336.

FOR ASSEMBLY

Carefully unmold and cut the brioche in half horizontally. Use a pastry bag fitted with a size 20 plain tip to pipe balls of crème diplomat all over the surface of the lower half of the brioche. Cover with the top half.

71

SAKURA

For the cherry blossom ganache

●

4 ⅓ cups (1 kg) whipping cream

5¼ extra-large (UK large/100 g) egg
yolks (⅓ cup plus 1½ tablespoons)

¼ cup (50 g) superfine (caster)
sugar

3¾ teaspoons (21 g) gelatin mass
(1 teaspoon/3 g gelatin powder
hydrated in 3¾ teaspoons/18 g
water)

½ cup (150 g) sakura (cherry
blossom) paste

1¾ cups (400 g) mascarpone cheese

For the joconde cake

●

3 medium (UK small/140 g) eggs

⅞ cup (105 g) confectioners'
(icing) sugar

1⅛ cups (105 g) ground almonds

½ cup (50 g) sakura (cherry
blossom) tea powder

¼ cup (30 g) all-purpose (plain)
flour

1½ tablespoons (20 g) unsalted
butter, melted

2¾ large (UK medium/90 g) egg
whites (⅜ cup)

3¾ teaspoons (15 g) superfine
(caster) sugar

¼ cup (25 g) grapefruit zest

For the yuzu and tea gel

●

2 cups (500 g) lemon juice

5 tablespoons (30 g) hojicha
(roasted green tea)

¼ cup (50 g) superfine sugar

1 tablespoon (8 g) agar powder

1 teaspoon (3 g) xanthan gum

⅔ cup (150 g) candied yuzu

For the pink chocolate coating

●

See page 338

For the white chocolate coating

●

See page 338

For finishing

●

Non-melting snow white topping
sugar, such as Codineige or King
Arthur

FOR THE CHERRY BLOSSOM GANACHE

In a saucepan, bring the cream to a boil. Beat the yolks with the superfine sugar. Pour a little boiling cream over this mixture, then return it to the saucepan to make a crème anglaise. Cook for 2 minutes, then incorporate the gelatin mass and sakura paste using an immersion (stick) blender. Filter through a conical sieve, incorporate the mascarpone, and refrigerate for about 12 hours.

FOR THE JOCONDE CAKE

Preheat the oven to 350°F (175°C/Gas Mark 4). In a stand mixer fitted with the whisk attachment, beat the eggs with the confectioners' sugar, ground almonds, and sakura tea powder. Incorporate the flour and melted butter. Beat the egg whites until stiff with the superfine sugar, then add the grapefruit zest. Fold the beaten egg whites into the batter. Spread the batter over a baking sheet lined with a Silpat mat and bake for 10 minutes. Let cool. Use a 6¼-inch (16-cm)-diameter pastry ring to cut out a disk from the joconde cake.

FOR THE YUZU AND TEA GEL

In a saucepan, bring the lemon juice to a boil. Add the tea and let boil for 5 minutes, then incorporate the superfine sugar, agar, and xanthan gum using an immersion blender. Refrigerate until set, then blend again. Mix in the candied yuzu.

FOR THE PINK AND WHITE CHOCOLATE COATINGS

Make the pink chocolate coating and the white chocolate coating as described on page 338.

FOR ASSEMBLY

Whip the ganache with a hand mixer. Arrange a 6¼-inch (16-cm)-diameter pastry ring lined with an acetate strip over the cake. Spread a layer of gel over the cake, smoothing as much as possible. Freeze for about 6 hours. Pipe ganache over the entire surface of a 7-inch (18-cm)-diameter Pavoni silicone entremets mold. Pipe more in the middle so the insert will be well centered. Introduce the insert, cover with ganache, and smooth with a spatula (palette knife). Freeze for about 6 hours, until set.

FOR FINISHING

Use a pastry (piping) bag fitted with a size 104 Saint-Honoré tip (nozzle) to pipe ganache flowers. First, pipe a tiny ball of ganache, freeze it until set, then insert a toothpick (cocktail stick) into it. Next, pipe five small petals onto the ball and finish with tiny upright lines to make the pistils of the flower. Freeze until set. Use a spray gun to flock the flowers with white chocolate coating, then spray a fine layer of pink chocolate coating to the tips. Make an attractive arrangement with the flowers on the entremets and dust them with a thin layer of snow sugar.

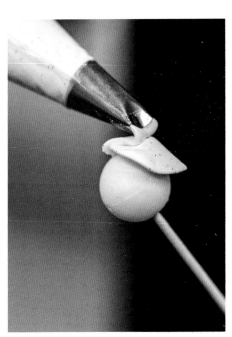

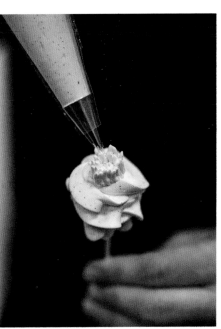

PPPY

For the raw cream ganache

⅞ cup (200 g) whipping cream

5 large (UK medium/85 g) egg yolks

3½ tablespoons (40 g) superfine (caster) sugar

1 tablespoon (17 g) gelatin mass (¾ teaspoon/2.5 g gelatin powder hydrated in 1 tablespoon/14.5 g water)

1 ⅓ cups (330 g) mascarpone cheese

⅔ cup (150 g) raw crème fraîche

¼ teaspoon (1 g) charcoal black food coloring

For the choux pastry sponge cake

2 teaspoons (10 g) milk

1¾ tablespoons (25 g) unsalted butter

¼ cup plus 1½ teaspoons (35 g) cake (Italian "00") flour

1 medium (UK small/45 g) egg

2 extra-large (UK large/40 g) egg yolks

2 extra-large (UK large/80 g) egg whites

¼ cup (55 g) superfine (caster) sugar

10 fresh strawberries

For the strawberry and poppy gel

1 ⅔ cups (400 g) strawberry juice

3½ tablespoons (40 g) superfine (caster) sugar

2¼ teaspoons (6 g) agar powder

¾ teaspoon (2 g) xanthan gum

1¾ teaspoons (5 g) crystallized poppy petals

For the almond and poppy seed crisp

3 tablespoons (35 g) superfine (caster) sugar

1⅞ cups (100 g) feuilletine flakes

⅔ cup (100 g) whole almonds

2 tablespoons (20 g) poppy seeds

2 teaspoons (10 g) grapeseed oil

2¼ teaspoons (10 g) cocoa butter, melted

For the ruby glaze

1¾ cups (400 g) whipping cream

2 teaspoons (6 g) potato starch

2½ tablespoons (42 g) gelatin mass (1⅞ teaspoons/6 g gelatin powder hydrated in 2½ tablespoons/36 g water)

1 teaspoon (5 g) red fat-soluble food coloring

For the ruby chocolate coating

See page 338

For assembly and finishing

Poppy seeds

FOR THE RAW CREAM GANACHE

Bring the whipping cream to a boil. Beat the yolks with the sugar. Pour a little boiling cream over this mixture, then return it to the saucepan to make a crème anglaise. Cook for 2 minutes, then incorporate the gelatin mass using an immersion (stick) blender. Filter through a conical sieve and add the mascarpone and raw crème fraîche. Refrigerate for 12 hours. Mix ¾ cup (150 g) ganache with the food coloring. Refrigerate.

FOR THE CHOUX PASTRY SPONGE

Preheat the oven to 325°F (165°C/Gas Mark 3). In a saucepan, combine the milk with the butter and bring to a boil. Let boil for 1-2 minutes, then add the flour and stir over low heat until the paste pulls away easily from the sides of the pan. Transfer to a stand mixer fitted with a flat beater attachment. Mix to release the steam, then add the eggs and yolks in three batches. Beat the egg whites until stiff, adding the sugar in three batches. The meringue is ready when it forms a peak on the end of the whisk without collapsing. Fold the meringue into the choux paste in three batches until incorporated and smooth. Pipe the batter into a 7-inch (18-cm)-diameter pastry ring. Cut the strawberries and insert them into the batter. Bake for 20-25 minutes, opening the oven door halfway through cooking to prevent condensation. Let cool.

FOR THE STRAWBERRY AND POPPY GEL

In a saucepan, bring the strawberry juice to a boil, then add the sugar, agar, and xanthan gum. Incorporate using an immersion (stick) blender and refrigerate until set. Blend in the poppy petals.

FOR THE ALMOND AND POPPY SEED CRISP

Make 1½ tablespoons (30 g) dry caramel with the sugar. Let cool until solid. Use an immersion blender to process, separately, the feuilletine flakes, followed by the caramel with the almonds and poppy seeds while gradually incorporating the oil. In a stand mixer fitted with a flat beater attachment, mix all the ingredients together while gradually adding the melted cocoa butter.

FOR THE RUBY GLAZE

Bring the cream to a boil. Add the starch and bring back to a boil. Incorporate the gelatin mass and the coloring using an immersion blender, then filter through a conical sieve.

FOR THE RUBY CHOCOLATE COATING

Make the ruby chocolate coating as described on page 338.

FOR ASSEMBLY

Whip the ganache with a hand mixer. Carefully lift off the pastry ring from the sponge. Place it in another pastry ring of the same diameter previously lined with a thin layer of the crisp. Cover everything with the gel, without letting the insert exceed 1 inch (2.5 cm) in height. Freeze for 4 hours. Pipe ganache over the entire surface of a 7-inch (18-cm)-diameter Pavoni silicone entremets mold. Pipe more in the middle so the insert will be well centered. Add the insert and cover with ganache. Smooth with a spatula (palette knife). Freeze for about 6 hours, until set. Place the entremets on a wire rack and glaze with the ruby glaze. Decorate around the sides with poppy seeds.

FOR FiNiSHiNG

Use a pastry (piping) bag fitted with a size 104 Saint-Honoré tip (nozzle) to pipe flowers with four large petals over the reverse side of 1¾-inch (4.5-cm)-diameter hemispherical silicone mold cavities. Freeze until set, then carefully unmold and turn the flowers over. Use a spray gun to uniformly flock the flowers with ruby chocolate coating. Arrange them on the entremets mold. Whip the black ganache with a hand mixer. Use a pastry bag fitted with a size 2 plain tip to make the poppy pistils by piping upright lines in raw cream ganache, then pipe upright lines of black ganache around the pistils. Decorate with poppy seeds. Refrigerate for about 4 hours before serving.

CROQUEM-BOUCHE

For the choux puffs

⅞ cup (200 g) milk

1⅜ teaspoons (8 g) salt

4 teaspoons (16 g) superfine (caster) sugar

¾ cup plus 1 tablespoon (1⅝ sticks/180 g) unsalted butter

1⅔ cups (220 g) bread (strong) flour

6¾ large (UK medium/360 g) eggs (1½ cups)

Pearl sugar

For the vanilla pastry cream

1¾ cups (420 g) milk

⅓ cup (75 g) whipping cream

1 vanilla bean (pod)

8 large (UK medium/135 g) egg yolks

⅝ cup (120 g) superfine sugar

2 tablespoons (36 g) custard powder

3 tablespoons (45 g) unsalted butter, softened

⅓ cup plus 1 tablespoon (90 g) mascarpone cheese

For the Saint-Honoré caramel

●

¼ ounce (8 g) dry nougat

1¾ teaspoons (8 g) glucose powder

2½ tablespoons (30 g) superfine (caster) sugar

1¼ cups (250 g) isomalt

For the nougatine

2½ cups (500 g) superfine (caster) sugar

2¼ cups (500 g) glucose powder

2¾ cups (400 g) crushed almonds

FOR THE CHOUX PUFFS

In a saucepan, combine ⅞ cup (200 g) water with the milk, salt, sugar, and butter and bring to a boil. Let boil for 1-2 minutes, then add the flour and stir over low heat until the paste pulls away easily from the sides of the pan. Transfer to a stand mixer fitted with a flat beater attachment. Mix to release the steam, then add the eggs in three batches. Refrigerate for about 2 hours. On a baking sheet lined with a Silpain perforated baking mat, pipe 2-2½-inch (5-6-cm)-diameter choux puffs. Sprinkle pearl sugar over one-quarter of the puffs. Bake in a deck oven at 350°F (175°C) for 30 minutes. (Or bake in a conventional oven: Preheat the oven to 500°F/260°C/Gas Mark 10, introduce the baking sheet, and turn off the oven for 15 minutes, then turn it back on and continue baking at 325°F/160°C/Gas Mark 3 for 10 minutes). Let cool.

FOR THE VANILLA PASTRY CREAM

In a saucepan, combine the milk with the cream and bring to a boil. Add the split and scraped vanilla bean and seeds, then remove from the heat. Cover and let infuse for about 10 minutes. Bring back to a boil, then filter through a conical sieve. In the meantime, using a whisk, beat the yolks in a large bowl with the sugar and custard powder until thick and pale. Pour the boiling mixture over the yolk mixture. Let boil for 2 minutes before incorporating the butter and mascarpone. Fill the choux puffs with plenty of pastry cream.

FOR THE SAINT-HONORÉ CARAMEL

Mix the dry nougat with 1 tablespoon (15 g) water and the glucose. Combine in a saucepan with the sugar and place over the heat. Heat the isomalt in another saucepan. When the isomalt reaches 300°F (150°C), incorporate it into the sugar mixture and cook to a dark caramel.

FOR THE NOUGATINE

In a saucepan, combine the sugar and glucose and heat to 365°F (185°C). Add the crushed almonds and let caramelize for about 2 minutes. Pour the nougatine into 7-inch (18-cm)-diameter flower-shape pastry rings on a Silpat mat. Let set at room temperature.

FOR ASSEMBLY

Insert a toothpick (cocktail stick) into the plain choux puffs (without pearl sugar) and dip the rounded sides into the hot caramel. Let cool for a few seconds. Attach the choux puffs along the edge of each nougatine flower with their rounded sides facing outward. Make a ring, alternating the caramel-dipped choux puffs with the sugar-coated ones. Position another nougatine flower on top and repeat the process to create the croquembouche.

LAVENDER

For the lavender ganache

3⅓ cups (800 g) whipping cream

1 cup (25 g) culinary lavender

7½ ounces (215 g) white couverture chocolate, chopped

2½ teaspoons (14 g) gelatin mass (⅝ teaspoon/2 g gelatin powder hydrated in 2½ teaspoons/12 g water)

For the baba batter

See page 341

For the baba soaking syrup

See page 343

For the apricot preserves

2⅓ cups (600 g) apricot puree

2¼ teaspoons (6 g) xanthan gum

1½ teaspoons (6 g) ascorbic acid

1¼ cups (200 g) cubed apricots

For the lavender glaze

⅓ cup (100 g) neutral glaze

⅜ ounce (10 g) fresh lavender flowers

For the blue chocolate coating

½ cup (100 g) cocoa butter

3½ ounces (100 g) white chocolate, chopped

½ teaspoon (2 g) blue fat-soluble food coloring

¼ teaspoon (1 g) charcoal black food coloring

FOR THE LAVENDER GANACHE

The previous day, heat half the cream in a saucepan with the lavender. Remove from the heat and let infuse, covered, for 5 minutes. Bring back to a boil while processing the cream using an immersion (stick) blender. Pour it over the chopped chocolate and gelatin mass. Incorporate using the immersion blender, adding the remaining cream, until the ganache is smooth. Refrigerate for about 12 hours.

FOR THE BABA BATTER

Preheat the oven to 350°F (175°C/Gas Mark 4). Make the baba batter as described on page 341.

Put the batter into a loaf pan. Bake at 350°F (180°C/Gas Mark 4) for 15 minutes, then at 325°F (160°C/Gas Mark 3) for 15 minutes, and finally at 275°F (140°C/Gas Mark 1) for 6 minutes.

FOR THE BABA SOAKING SYRUP

Make the baba soaking syrup as described on page 343.

FOR THE APRICOT MARMALADE

Blend the puree with the xanthan gum and ascorbic acid. Mix in the apricot cubes and refrigerate.

FOR THE LAVENDER GLAZE

In a saucepan, bring the neutral glaze with the lavender flowers to a boil, then mix well.

FOR THE BLUE CHOCOLATE COATING

Melt and pour the cocoa butter over the chopped chocolate. Incorporate the food colorings using an immersion blender until smooth.

FOR ASSEMBLY

In a saucepan, heat the syrup to 144°F (62°C) and immerse the baba completely. Soak for 12 hours. The next day, take the baba out of the syrup and return it to the loaf pan. Spread with a layer of apricot preserves. Freeze for about 4 hours, until set.

FOR FINISHING

Carefully unmold the cake. Whip the ganache with a hand mixer. Use a pastry (piping) bag fitted with a size 104 Saint-Honoré tip (nozzle) to pipe long lines of whipped ganache along the entire length of the cake, leaving a hollow space in the center. Lightly jerk your wrist at the end of each line to curl the tip. Use a spray gun to cover the cake uniformly with the blue chocolate coating. Fill the center with the lavender glaze.

RASPBERRY

LUNETTE

For the Viennese shortbread

●

1 vanilla bean (pod)

⅞ cup plus 1 tablespoon (1⅞ sticks/
210 g) unsalted butter, softened

¾ teaspoon (3 g) fleur de sel

½ cup plus 1 tablespoon (70 g)
confectioners' (icing) sugar,
sifted

1¼ large (UK medium/40 g) egg
whites (2 tablespoons plus
2 teaspoons)

2 cups (250 g) all-purpose (plain)
flour, sifted

For the raspberry preserves

●

3⅛ cups (475 g) fully ripe
raspberries

¼ cup plus 1 tablespoon (70 g)
raspberry juice

¾ cup (145 g) superfine (caster)
sugar

¼ cup (50 g) glucose powder

2½ teaspoons (10 g) pectin NH

½ teaspoon (3 g) tartaric acid

FOR THE VIENNESE SHORTBREAD

Preheat the oven to 325°F (165°C/Gas Mark 3). Split the vanilla bean (pod),
scrape out the seeds, and roast the bean in the oven for 20 minutes.
Grind the roasted bean to a fine powder. Use a spatula (palette knife) to
mix the softened butter with the salt and vanilla seeds and powder. Add,
in succession, the sifted confectioners' sugar, egg whites, and sifted
flour. Mix to a smooth batter. Raise the oven temperature to 340°F (170°C/
Gas Mark 3½). Divide the batter and pipe half over the bottom of a 7-inch
(18-cm)-diameter flower-shape baking pan. Pipe the other half into an
identical pan. Put the two pans into the oven and bake for about 20 minutes.
If you only have one pan, bake one after the other. Use a cookie cutter to
cut out teardrop-shape holes from one of the shortbread flowers, one inside
each of the petals. Create a flower in the center made up of eight teardrops.

FOR THE RASPBERRY PRESERVES

Cook the raspberries for about 30 minutes, until soft, while gradually
adding the raspberry juice. Add the superfine sugar, glucose powder, pectin,
and tartaric acid, mix, and bring to a boil for 1 minute. Refrigerate until
set.

FOR ASSEMBLY

Spread a generous layer of raspberry preserves over the undecorated cookie,
leaving a margin around the edges uncovered to prevent overflowing. Cover
with the second cookie. Pipe preserves into each teardrop, filling the
middle ones more.

SUMMER

VANiLLA

For the vanilla ganache

See page 340

For the sweet tart shell

See page 342

For the vanilla crisp

See page 337

For the milk preserves

⅓ cup plus 1 tablespoon (120 g) sweetened condensed milk

2 teaspoons (4 g) vanilla pearls (or vanilla seeds)

½ cup (120 g) evaporated milk

¾ teaspoon (2 g) xanthan gum

¼ teaspoon (1 g) charcoal black food coloring

For the almond dacquoise

2½ large (UK medium/80 g) egg whites (⅓ cup)

3 tablespoons (35 g) superfine (caster) sugar

¾ cup (70 g) ground almonds

2 tablespoons (15 g) all-purpose (plain) flour

⅓ cup plus 2 tablespoons (55 g) confectioners' sugar

For the vanilla glaze

⅓ cup (100 g) neutral glaze

½ teaspoon (1 g) vanilla pearls (or vanilla seeds)

FOR THE VANILLA GANACHE

Make the vanilla ganache as described on page 340.

FOR THE SWEET TART SHELL

Make the sweet tart shell (case) as described on page 342.

FOR THE VANILLA CRISP

Make the vanilla crisp as described on page 337.

FOR THE MILK PRESERVES

In a copper saucepan, caramelize the condensed milk in the oven at 195°F (90°C) for 4 hours. Let cool, then transfer to a food processor. Add the vanilla pearls, evaporated milk, xanthan gum, and food coloring and blend until the mixture thickens.

FOR THE ALMOND DACQUOISE

Preheat the oven to 340°F (170°C/Gas Mark 3½). Make a French meringue by beating the egg whites until stiff, incorporating the superfine sugar in three batches. The meringue is ready when it forms a peak on the end of the whisk without collapsing. Fold in the superfine sugar, ground almonds, flour, and confectioners' sugar. Pipe the dacquoise batter into an 8-inch (20-cm)-diameter pastry ring and bake for 16 minutes.

FOR ASSEMBLY

Fill the tart shell halfway with vanilla crisp. Fill to four-fifths with the milk preserves. Lift off the pastry ring from the dacquoise and reduce its diameter by ⅜-¾ inch (1-2 cm) to make piping easier. Insert the dacquoise disk, leaving it flush with the top edge of the tart shell.

FOR FINISHING

Whip the ganache with a hand mixer. Using a metal stand and a pastry (piping) bag fitted with a size 125 Saint-Honoré tip (nozzle), pipe irregular petals in whipped ganache. To do this, hold the vanilla flower in one hand and tilt it by about 20 degrees, then use your other hand to pipe in a circular motion, folding over into the middle with a perpendicular stroke to form what appears to be the "tips" of the petals.

FOR THE VANILLA GLAZE

In a saucepan, combine the neutral glaze with the vanilla pearls and bring to a boil. Transfer the mixture to a spray gun and flock the tart with glaze.

FRAMBOiSiER WiTH PETALS

For the choux pastry sponge

2 teaspoons (10 g) milk

1¾ tablespoons (25 g) unsalted butter

¼ cup plus 1½ teaspoons (35 g) cake (Italian "00") flour

1 medium (UK small/45 g) egg

2⅓ large (UK medium/40 g) egg yolks (2 tablespoons plus 2 teaspoons)

2⅓ large (UK medium/80 g) egg whites (⅓ cup)

¼ cup (55 g) superfine (caster) sugar

10 fresh raspberries

For the vanilla pastry cream

½ cup (120 g) milk

4 teaspoons (20 g) whipping cream

1 vanilla bean (pod)

2⅓ large (UK medium/40 g) egg yolks (2 tablespoons plus 2 teaspoons)

3 tablespoons (35 g) superfine (caster) sugar

1¾ teaspoons (10 g) custard powder

1 tablespoon (15 g) unsalted butter, softened

2 tablespoons (30 g) mascarpone cheese

For the vanilla ganache

2⅔ cups (625 g) whipping cream

1 vanilla bean (pod)

5 ounces (140 g) white couverture chocolate

2 tablespoons (35 g) gelatin mass (1½ teaspoons/5 g gelatin powder hydrated in 2 tablespoons/30 g water)

For the crème diplomat

See page 336

For the aged raspberries

2½ cups (300 g) fresh raspberries

2½ tablespoons (30 g) superfine (caster) sugar

For the raspberry gel

See page 341

For the ruby chocolate coating

See page 338

For assembly

¼ lime

4 cups (500 g) fresh raspberries

FOR THE CHOUX PASTRY SPONGE

Preheat the oven to 325°F (165°C/Gas Mark 3). In a saucepan, combine the milk with the butter and bring to a boil. Let boil for 1-2 minutes, then add the flour and stir over low heat until the paste pulls away easily from the sides of the pan. Transfer to a stand mixer fitted with a flat beater attachment. Mix to release the steam, then gradually add the eggs and yolks in three batches. Beat the egg whites until stiff, adding the sugar in three batches. The meringue is ready when it forms a peak on the end of the whisk without collapsing. Fold the meringue into the choux paste in three batches until incorporated and smooth. Pipe the batter into an 8-inch (20-cm)-diameter pastry ring. Insert the raspberries into the batter, then bake for 20-25 minutes, opening the oven door halfway through baking to prevent condensation. Let cool.

FOR THE VANILLA PASTRY CREAM

Make the vanilla pastry cream as described on page 336.

FOR THE VANILLA GANACHE

Make the vanilla ganache as described on page 340.

FOR THE CRÈME DIPLOMAT

Make the crème diplomate as described on page 336.

FOR THE AGED RASPBERRIES

Wash and hull the raspberries. Arrange them in a dish and sprinkle the sugar over them. Cover with a lid, then cover with plastic wrap (clingfilm). If the dish does not have a lid, cover it with two layers of plastic wrap. It must be wrapped tightly for an airtight seal. Cook in a bain-marie or steam oven at 210°F (100°C) for 1 hour 15 minutes. Collect the juice released by the raspberries to make the gel.

FOR THE RASPBERRY GEL

Make the raspberry gel as described on page 341.

FOR THE RUBY CHOCOLATE COATING

Make the ruby chocolate coating as described on page 338.

FOR ASSEMBLY

Carefully lift off the pastry ring from the sponge. Replace it with another pastry ring of the same size lined with an acetate strip. The strip should be ⅜-¾ inch (1-2 cm) wider than the height of the pastry ring. Fill a pastry bag with the crème diplomat and pipe a thin layer over the sponge. Pipe more cream around the edges to fill completely and smooth with a small spatula (palette knife). Arrange aged raspberries over the crème diplomat at the center of the cake. Process half of the raspberry gel using an immersion (stick) blender and pipe it into the gaps, leaving an almost completely smooth surface. Set aside some of this gel for later. Cut the remaining unprocessed gel into cubes and spread them over the center of the cake. Grate the lime zest with a Microplane (fine grater). By the time the cake is assembled thus far, the top should be about ¼ inch (5 mm) below the top edge of the acetate. Finish with a layer of crème diplomat. Smooth with a spatula. Freeze for about 30 minutes, until set, then pipe a thin layer of raspberry gel over the top. Smooth with a spatula.

FOR FINISHING

Whip the ganache with a hand mixer. Use a pastry (piping) bag fitted with a size 104 Saint-Honoré tip (nozzle) to pipe ganache over the sides of the cake. Pipe diagonal lines starting at the top of the cake and finishing at the bottom. Transfer the ruby chocolate coating to a spray gun and lightly flock the side of the cake for a speckled effect. Halve the raspberries and arrange them in concentric circles over the top of the cake, leaving a space in the middle. Fill the space with raspberry gel.

WiLD STRAWBERRY

For the joconde cake

See page 335

For the vanilla pastry cream

½ cup (120 g) milk

4 teaspoons (20 g) whipping cream

1 vanilla bean (pod)

2⅓ large (UK medium/40 g) egg yolks
(2 tablespoons plus 2 teaspoons)

3 tablespoons (35 g) superfine
(caster) sugar

1¾ teaspoons (10 g) custard powder

1 tablespoon (15 g) unsalted
butter, softened

2 tablespoons (30 g) mascarpone
cheese

For the vanilla ganache

2⅔ cups (625 g) whipping cream

1 vanilla bean (pod)

5 ounces (140 g) white couverture
chocolate

2 tablespoons (35 g) gelatin mass
(1½ teaspoons/5 g gelatin powder
hydrated in 2 tablespoons/30 g
water)

For the crème diplomat

See page 336

For the aged strawberries

2 cups (300 g) strawberries

2½ tablespoons (30 g) superfine
(caster) sugar

For the strawberry gel

See page 340

For the ruby chocolate coating

See page 338

For assembly

¼ lime

3¼ cups (500 g) wild strawberries

103

FOR THE JOCONDE CAKE

Make the joconde cake as described on page 335.

FOR THE VANILLA PASTRY CREAM

Make the vanilla pastry cream as described on page 336.

FOR THE VANILLA GANACHE

Make the vanilla ganache as described on page 340.

CRÈME DIPLOMAT

Make the crème diplomate as described on page 336.

FOR THE AGED STRAWBERRIES

Wash and hull the strawberries. Arrange them in a dish and sprinkle the sugar over them. Cover with a lid, then cover with plastic wrap (clingfilm). If the dish does not have a lid, cover it with two layers of plastic wrap. It must be wrapped tightly for an airtight seal. Cook in a bain-marie or steam oven at 210°F (100°C) for about 1 hour 15 minutes. Collect the juice released by the strawberries to make the gel.

FOR THE STRAWBERRY GEL

Make the strawberry gel as described on page 340.

FOR THE RUBY CHOCOLATE COATING

Make the ruby chocolate coating as described on page 338.

FOR ASSEMBLY

Carefully lift off the pastry ring from the sponge. Replace it with another pastry ring of the same size lined with an acetate strip. The strip should be ⅜-¾ inch (1-2 cm) wider than the height of the pastry ring. Fill a pastry bag with the crème diplomat and pipe a thin layer over the sponge. Pipe more cream around the edges to fill completely and smooth with a small spatula (palette knife). Arrange the aged strawberries over the crème diplomat at the center of the cake. Process half of the strawberry gel using an immersion (stick) blender and pipe it into the gaps, leaving an almost completely smooth surface. Set aside some of this gel for later. Cut the remaining unprocessed gel into cubes and spread them over the center of the cake. Grate the lime zest with a Microplane (fine grater). By the time the cake is assembled thus far, the top should be about ¼ inch (5 mm) below the top edge of the acetate. Finish with a layer of crème diplomat. Smooth with a spatula. Freeze for about 30 minutes, until set, then pipe a thin layer of strawberry gel over the top. Smooth with a spatula.

FiNiSHiNG

Whip the ganache with a hand mixer. Cut off the end off a tipless pastry (piping) bag and improvise a Saint-Honoré tip (nozzle) by cutting a ⅛-inch (3-mm) notch. Starting at the top of the cake, pipe small, even flames of ganache in concentric rings over the sides. Use a spray gun to uniformly flock the cake with ruby chocolate coating. Arrange the wild strawberries at the center of the cake.

CHERRY TREE

For the choux pastry sponge

2 teaspoons (10 g) milk

1¾ tablespoons (25 g) unsalted butter

¼ cup plus 1½ teaspoons (35 g) cake (Italian "00") flour

1 medium (UK small/45 g) egg

2⅓ large (UK medium/40 g) egg yolks (2 tablespoons plus 2 teaspoons)

2⅓ large (UK medium/80 g) egg whites (⅓ cup)

¼ cup (55 g) superfine (caster) sugar

10 fresh cherries, pitted and halved

For the crème diplomat

See page 336

For the aged cherries

2⅛ cups (300 g) fresh cherries

2½ tablespoons (30 g) superfine sugar

For the vanilla pastry cream

½ cup (120 g) milk

4 teaspoons (20 g) whipping cream

1 vanilla bean (pod)

2⅓ large (UK medium/40 g) egg yolks (2 tablespoons plus 2 teaspoons)

3 tablespoons (35 g) superfine (caster) sugar

1¾ teaspoons (10 g) custard powder

1 tablespoon (15 g) unsalted butter, softened

2 tablespoons (30 g) mascarpone cheese

For the cherry gel

1½ cups (400 g) cherry juice

3½ tablespoons (40 g) superfine (caster) sugar

2¼ teaspoons (6 g) agar powder

¾ teaspoon (2 g) xanthan gum

For the vanilla ganache

2⅔ cups (625 g) whipping cream

1 vanilla bean (pod)

5 ounces (140 g) white couverture chocolate

2 tablespoons (35 g) gelatin mass (1½ teaspoons/5 g gelatin powder hydrated in 2 tablespoons/30 g water)

For assembly

¼ lime

3⅔ cups (500 g) ripe cherries

For the vanilla glaze

⅓ cup (100 g) neutral glaze

½ teaspoon (1 g) vanilla pearls (or vanilla seeds)

FOR THE CHOUX PASTRY SPONGE

Preheat the oven to 325°F (165°C/Gas Mark 3). In a saucepan, combine the milk with the butter and bring to a boil. Let boil for 1-2 minutes, then add the flour and stir over low heat until the paste pulls away easily from the sides of the pan. Transfer to a stand mixer fitted with a flat beater attachment. Mix to release the steam, then gradually add the eggs and yolks in three batches. Beat the egg whites until stiff, adding the sugar in three batches. The meringue is ready when it forms a peak on the end of the whisk without collapsing. Fold the meringue into the choux paste in three batches until incorporated and smooth. Pipe the batter into an 8-inch (20-cm)-diameter pastry ring. Insert the cherries into the batter, then bake for 20-25 minutes, opening the oven door halfway through baking to prevent condensation. Let cool.

FOR THE VANILLA PASTRY CREAM

Make the vanilla pastry cream as described on page 336.

FOR THE VANILLA GANACHE

Make the vanilla ganache as described on page 340.

FOR THE CRÈME DIPLOMAT

Make the crème diplomate as described on page 336.

FOR THE AGED CHERRIES

Wash, remove the stems, and pit (stone) the cherries. Arrange the cherries in a dish and sprinkle the sugar over them. Cover with a lid, then cover with plastic wrap (clingfilm). If the dish does not have a lid, cover it with two layers of plastic wrap. It must be wrapped tightly for an airtight seal. Cook in a bain-marie or steam oven at 210°F (100°C) for about 1 hour 15 minutes. Collect the juice released by the cherries to make the gel.

FOR THE CHERRY GEL

In a saucepan, bring the cherry juice to a boil and then add the sugar, agar, and xanthan gum. Incorporate using an immersion (stick) blender and refrigerate until set.

FOR ASSEMBLY

Carefully lift off the pastry ring from the sponge. Replace it with another pastry ring of the same size lined with an acetate strip. The strip should be ⅜-¾ inch (1-2 cm) wider than the height of the pastry ring. Fill a pastry bag with the crème diplomat and pipe a thin layer over the sponge. Pipe more cream around the edges and smooth with a small spatula (palette knife) to completely fill the space. Arrange the aged cherries over the crème diplomat at the center of the cake. Process half of the cherry gel using an immersion blender and pipe it into the gaps, leaving an almost completely smooth surface. Set aside some of this gel for later. Cut the remaining unprocessed gel into cubes and spread them over the center of the cake. Grate the lime zest with a Microplane (fine grater). By the time the cake is assembled thus far, the top should be about ¼ inch (5 mm) below the top edge of the acetate. Finish with a layer of crème diplomat. Smooth with a spatula. Freeze for about 30 minutes, until set, then pipe a thin layer of cherry gel over the top. Smooth with a spatula.

FOR FINISHING

Whip the ganache with a hand mixer. Use a pastry (piping) bag fitted with a size 125 Saint-Honoré tip (nozzle) to pipe ganache over the sides of the cake. Pipe about 2½-inch (5-cm)-long curved lines to make a ring of petals around the top edge of the cake. Repeat the process to pipe the lower rings. The petals in the second ring should not exceed the width of the top petals by more than half their width. Make an attractive arrangement with the cherries, keeping the stems intact.

FOR THE VANILLA GLAZE

In a saucepan, combine the neutral glaze with the vanilla pearls and bring to a boil. Transfer the mixture to a spray gun and flock the tart with glaze.

FRAISIER

For the choux pastry sponge

2 teaspoons (10 g) milk

1¾ tablespoons (25 g) unsalted butter

¼ cup plus 1½ teaspoons (35 g) cake (Italian "00") flour

1 medium (UK small/45 g) egg

2⅓ large (UK medium/40 g) egg yolks (2 tablespoons plus 2 teaspoons)

2⅓ large (UK medium/80 g) egg whites (⅓ cup)

¼ cup (55 g) superfine (caster) sugar

10 fresh raspberries

For the vanilla ganache

3¼ cups (775 g) whipping cream

2 vanilla beans (pods)

6¼ ounces (175 g) white couverture chocolate

2 tablespoons plus 1¾ teaspoons (42 g) gelatin mass (1⅛ teaspoons/ 6 g gelatin powder hydrated in 2 tablespoons plus 1¾ teaspoons/ 36 g water)

For the strawberry gel

See page 340

For assembly

20 fresh strawberries

¼ lime

For the vanilla glaze and finishing

⅓ cup (100 g) neutral glaze

½ teaspoon (1 g) vanilla pearls (or vanilla seeds)

2 cups (300 g) fresh strawberries (red, white, or pink)

FOR THE CHOUX PASTRY SPONGE

Preheat the oven to 325°F (165°C/Gas Mark 3). In a saucepan, combine the milk with the butter and bring to a boil. Let boil for 1-2 minutes, then add the flour and stir over low heat until the paste pulls away easily from the sides of the pan. Transfer to a stand mixer fitted with a flat beater attachment. Mix to release the steam, then gradually add the eggs and yolks in three batches. Beat the egg whites until stiff, adding the sugar in three batches. The meringue is ready when it forms a peak on the end of the whisk without collapsing. Fold the meringue into the choux paste in three batches until incorporated and smooth. Pipe the batter into an 8-inch (20-cm)-diameter pastry ring. Insert the raspberries into the batter, then bake for 20-25 minutes, opening the oven door halfway through baking to prevent condensation. Let cool.

FOR THE VANILLA GANACHE

Make the vanilla ganache as described on page 340.

FOR THE STRAWBERRY GEL

Make the strawberry gel as described on page 340.

FOR ASSEMBLY

Whip the ganache with a hand mixer. Wash, hull, and thinly slice the strawberries. Carefully lift off the pastry ring from the sponge. Replace it with another pastry ring of the same size lined with an acetate strip. The strip should be ⅜-¾ inch (1-2 cm) wider than the height of the pastry ring. Fill a pastry bag with the strawberry gel and pipe a thin layer over the sponge. Pipe a ring of ganache around the edge, then smooth with a spatula (palette knife) to completely fill the space. Arrange the strawberry slices in the center of the cake and cover with a layer of gel. Grate the lime zest with a Microplane (fine grater). Cover with ganache until flush with the top of the acetate strip and smooth with a spatula. Freeze for about 1 hour.

FOR PIPING

Use a pastry (piping) bag fitted with a size 14 smooth basketweave tip (nozzle) to pipe lines of ganache around the strawberries. Start at the top and work your way downward for an even draped effect. Flick your wrist slightly backward to make a circular shape at the top of the cake.

FOR THE VANILLA GLAZE AND FINISHING

In a saucepan, combine the neutral glaze with the vanilla pearls and bring to a boil. Transfer the mixture to a spray gun and flock the tart with glaze. Make an attractive arrangement with the strawberries over the center of the cake, taking advantage of the different varieties and colors. To accentuate the contrast, leave a few strawberries unhulled at the top.

STRAWBERRY

For the diamond shortbread tart shell

See page 342

For the almond and vanilla cream

See page 336

For the vanilla pastry cream

●

1 cup (230 g) milk

3 tablespoons (40 g) whipping cream

1 vanilla bean (pod)

4 large (UK medium/70 g) egg yolks

¼ cup plus 1 tablespoon (60 g) superfine sugar

3½ teaspoons (20 g) custard powder

1¾ cups (25 g) unsalted butter, softened

3½ tablespoons (50 g) mascarpone cheese

For the aged strawberries

2 cups (300 g) fresh strawberries

2½ tablespoons (30 g) superfine sugar

For the strawberry gel

See page 341

For assembly

●

4 cups (600 g) fresh strawberries

FOR THE DIAMOND SHORTBREAD TART SHELL

Make the tart shell (case) as described on page 342.

FOR THE ALMOND AND VANILLA CREAM

Make the almond and vanilla cream as described on page 336.

FOR THE VANILLA PASTRY CREAM

Make the vanilla pastry cream as described on page 336.

FOR THE AGED STRAWBERRIES

Wash and hull the strawberries. Arrange them in a dish and sprinkle the sugar over them. Cover with a lid, then cover with plastic wrap (clingfilm). If the dish does not have a lid, cover it with two layers of plastic wrap. It must be wrapped tightly for an airtight seal. Cook in a bain-marie or steam oven at 210°F (100°C) for about 1 hour 15 minutes. Collect the juice released by the strawberries to make the gel.

FOR THE STRAWBERRY GEL

Make the strawberry gel as described on page 341.

FOR ASSEMBLY

Preheat the oven to 340°F (170°C/Gas Mark 3½). Fill the tart shell with almond and vanilla cream. Bake for 8 minutes and let cool for about 15 minutes. Add a thin layer of pastry cream. Fill the tart to three-quarters full with the pastry cream. Arrange the aged strawberries evenly and fill the tart completely with strawberry gel. Wash and hull the strawberries and cut vertically into thin slices. Make the first ring at the edge of the tart by laying the strawberries flat, then tilt them at a gradually increasing angle until the strawberry slices at the center are practically upright.

CHARLOTTE WITH MIXED BERRIES

For the lemon ganache

See page 340

For the pain de Gênes cake

See page 335

For the mixed berry preserves

¾ cup (100 g) fresh raspberries

⅔ cup (100 g) fresh strawberries

1 cup (100 g) fresh red currants

3 tablespoons (45 g) strawberry puree

1 drizzle olive oil

2½ tablespoons (30 g) superfine (caster) sugar

2 tablespoons plus ¾ teaspoon (30 g) glucose powder

1½ teaspoons (6 g) pectin NH

⅜ teaspoon (2 g) tartaric acid

For the chocolate coating

½ cup (100 g) cocoa butter

1¾ ounces (50 g) milk chocolate, chopped

1¾ ounces (50 g) white chocolate, chopped

For assembly

20 fresh strawberries

For finishing

3½-4 cups (500 g) mixed fresh berries (red currants, gooseberries, wild strawberries, raspberries, blackberries, strawberries)

Non-melting snow white topping sugar, such as Codineige or King Arthur

FOR THE LEMON GANACHE

Make the lemon ganache as described on page 340.

FOR THE PAIN DE GÊNES CAKE

Make the pain de Gênes cake as described on page 335.

FOR THE MIXED FRUIT PRESERVES

In a saucepan, caramelize the berries and strawberry puree with the olive oil, then simmer over low heat for 30 minutes. Add the sugar, glucose, pectin, and tartaric acid. Mix well and bring to a boil for 1 minute. Refrigerate until set.

FOR THE CHOCOLATE COATING

Melt the cocoa butter and pour it over the two chopped chocolates. Incorporate using an immersion (stick) blender until smooth.

FOR ASSEMBLY

Wash and hull the strawberries. Cut into thin slices. Carefully lift off the pastry ring from the cake. Replace it with another pastry ring of the same size lined with an acetate strip. The strip should be ⅜-¾ inch (1-2 cm) wider than the height of the pastry ring. Use a pastry (piping) bag to cover the cake with a thin layer of the preserves. Pipe cream around the edges and smooth with a small spatula (palette knife) to completely fill the space. Arrange the strawberries at the center of the cake. Cover with a thick layer of preserves. Fill with ganache until flush with the top of the acetate strip. Smooth with a spatula. Freeze for about 1 hour.

FOR FINISHING

Whip the rest of the ganache with a hand mixer. Use a pastry (piping) bag fitted with a size 14 plain tip (nozzle) to pipe 2½-2¾-inch (6-7-cm)-high strips of ganache over a baking sheet lined with a Silpat mat. Freeze until set. Lightly trim the less attractive end of the frozen strips. Pipe thin lines of ganache over the sides of the cake to hold the frozen strips in place. Arrange the strips, one at a time, around the charlotte, combining ones with different shapes and sizes for an irregular but pleasing effect. There should not be spaces between the strips. Use a spray gun to flock the outside of the cake. The chocolate coating must be practically at a boil for this step. Lightly dust with snow sugar for a powdery effect. Fill the top of the charlotte with the fresh mixed berries. Refrigerate for about 2 hours before serving.

RASPBERRY

For the diamond shortbread tart shell

See page 342

For the almond and vanilla cream

See page 336

For the vanilla pastry cream

1 cup (230 g) milk

3 tablespoons (40 g) whipping cream

1 vanilla bean (pod)

4 large (UK medium/70 g) egg yolks

¼ cup plus 1 tablespoon (60 g) superfine sugar

3½ teaspoons (20 g) custard powder

1¾ cups (25 g) unsalted butter, softened

3½ tablespoons (50 g) mascarpone cheese

For the aged raspberries

2½ cups (300 g) fresh raspberries

2½ tablespoons (30 g) superfine (caster) sugar

For the raspberry gel

See page 341

For assembly

4 cups (500 g) fresh raspberries, rinsed and halved

FOR THE DIAMOND SHORTBREAD TART SHELL

Make the tart shell (case) as described on page 342.

FOR THE ALMOND AND VANILLA CREAM

Make the almond and vanilla cream as described on page 336.

FOR THE VANILLA PASTRY CREAM

Make the vanilla pastry cream as described on page 336.

FOR THE AGED RASPBERRIES

Rinse the raspberries. Arrange them in a dish and sprinkle the sugar over them. Cover with a lid, then cover with plastic wrap (clingfilm). If the dish does not have a lid, cover it with two layers of plastic wrap. It must be wrapped tightly for an airtight seal. Cook in a bain-marie or steam oven at 210°F (100°C) for about 1 hour 15 minutes. Collect the juice released by the raspberries to make the gel.

FOR THE RASPBERRY GEL

Make the raspberry gel as described on page 341.

FOR ASSEMBLY

Preheat the oven to 340°F (170°C/Gas Mark 3½). Fill the tart shell with almond and vanilla cream. Bake for 8 minutes and let cool for about 15 minutes. Add a thin layer of pastry cream. Fill the tart to three-quarters full with the pastry cream. Arrange the aged raspberries evenly and fill the tart completely with raspberry gel. Arrange the raspberries to form small flowers over the top of the tart.

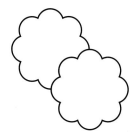

FRAMBOISIER

For the vanilla ganache

2 cups (625 g) whipping cream

1 vanilla bean (pod)

5 ounces (140 g) white couverture chocolate, chopped

2 tablespoons (35 g) gelatin mass (1½ teaspoons/5 g gelatin powder hydrated in 2 tablespoons/30 g water)

For the reconstituted Breton shortbread

See page 343

For the almond cream

See page 336

For the raspberry gel

See page 341

For the ruby chocolate coating

See page 338

For assembly

1¼ cups (150 g) fresh raspberries

FOR THE VANILLA GANACHE

Make the vanilla ganache as described on page 340.

FOR THE RECONSTITUTED BRETON SHORTBREAD

Make the reconstituted Breton shortbread as described on page 343.

FOR THE ALMOND CREAM

Make the almond cream as described on page 336.

FOR THE RASPBERRY GEL

Make the raspberry gel as described on page 341.

FOR THE RUBY CHOCOLATE COATING

Make the ruby chocolate coating as described on page 338.

FOR ASSEMBLY

Preheat the oven to 340°F (170°C/Gas Mark 3½). Whip the ganache with a hand mixer. Use a 6¼-inch (16-cm)-diameter pastry ring to trim the edges of the baked shortbread, then use a 5½-inch (14-cm)-diameter ring to cut out the center to create a ring of shortbread. Leave the two pastry rings in place. Pipe a layer of almond cream over the shortbread. Bake for about 8 minutes. Let cool for 15 minutes. Halve the raspberries, arrange them on top, and cover with gel. Freeze the insert for about 6 hours, until set. Pipe ganache over the entire inside surface of a 7-inch (18-cm)-diameter silicone bubble crown mold. Spread the ganache evenly over the edges, then introduce the insert, well centered. Finish with a layer of ganache and smooth with a spatula (palette knife). Freeze for at least 3 hours, until set, before carefully unmolding. Use a spray gun to uniformly flock the cake with ruby chocolate coating. Refrigerate for about 4 hours before serving.

BLACKBERRY

For the blackberry ganache

⅞ cup (200 g) whipping cream

5 large (UK medium/85 g) egg yolks

3½ tablespoons (40 g) superfine (caster) sugar

1 tablespoon (17 g) gelatin mass (¾ teaspoon/2.5 g gelatin powder hydrated in 1 tablespoon/14.5 g water)

1¼ cups (330 g) blackberry puree

1⅓ cups plus 1½ tablespoons (330 g) mascarpone cheese

For the clafoutis cake

2 extra-large (UK large/110 g) eggs

½ cup (100 g) superfine (caster) sugar

1 cup (100 g) ground almonds

¼ cup (30 g) all-purpose (plain) flour

scant ¼ teaspoon (1 g) salt

1¼ cups (300 g) crème fraîche

For the blackberry gel
●

1⅔ cups (400 g) blackberry juice

3½ tablespoons (40 g) superfine (caster) sugar

2¼ teaspoons (6 g) agar powder

¾ teaspoon (2 g) xanthan gum

For the charcoal black chocolate coating
●

See page 338

For assembly
●

3½ cups (500 g) fresh blackberries

132

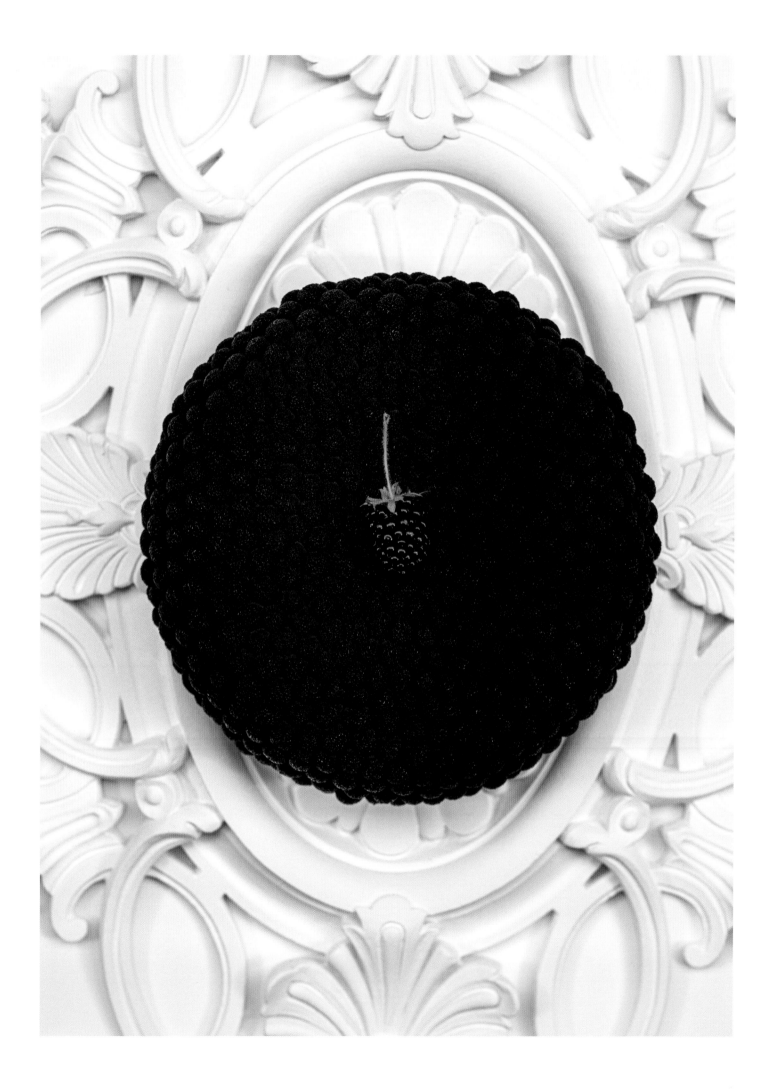

FOR THE BLACKBERRY GANACHE

In a saucepan, bring the cream to a boil. Beat the yolks with the sugar. Pour a little boiling cream over this mixture, then return it to the saucepan to make a crème anglaise. Cook for 2 minutes, then incorporate the gelatin mass and blackberry puree using an immersion (stick) blender. Filter through a conical sieve and add the mascarpone. Refrigerate for about 12 hours.

FOR THE CLAFOUTIS CAKE

Preheat the oven to 340°F (170°C/Gas Mark 3½). Mix the eggs with the sugar and ground almonds, then add the flour, salt, and crème fraîche. Pour the batter into a baking pan to a height of 2 inches (5 cm). Bake for about 15 minutes. Let cool, then cut out a 6¼-inch (16-cm)-diameter disk.

FOR THE BLACKBERRY GEL

In a saucepan, bring the blackberry juice to a boil, then add the sugar, agar, and xanthan gum. Incorporate using an immersion (stick) blender and refrigerate until set.

FOR THE CHARCOAL BLACK CHOCOLATE COATING

Make the charcoal black coating as described on page 338.

FOR ASSEMBLY

Whip the ganache with a hand mixer. Carefully lift off the pastry ring from the cake. Replace it with another pastry ring of the same size lined with an acetate strip. The strip should be ⅜–¾ inch (1–2 cm) wider than the height of the pastry ring. Spread a layer of gel over the cake, then arrange the whole blackberries over it. Cover with gel to the top of the blackberries, making the gel layer as smooth as possible. Freeze for about 6 hours. Pipe ganache over the entire surface of a 7-inch (18-cm)-diameter Pavoni silicone entremets mold. Pipe more in the middle so the insert will be well centered. Add the insert and cover with ganache. Smooth with a spatula (palette knife). Freeze until set, about 6 hours.

FOR FINISHING

Use a pastry (piping) bag fitted with an ⅛-inch (4-mm) plain tip (nozzle) to pipe small ganache balls one at a time, starting from the center of the cake. The aim is to pipe balls of identical size that are tightly packed together. You will need to take your time and be meticulous. Don't try to arrange them in any particular order; instead, pipe them in an irregular fashion over the surface of the cake. Use a spray gun to uniformly flock the cake with charcoal black chocolate coating. Refrigerate for about 4 hours before serving.

HAZLNUT

For the hazelnut ganache

¾ cup (170 g) whipping cream

1½ tablespoons (20 g) hazelnut paste

1¼ ounces (35 g) white couverture chocolate, chopped

1½ tablespoons (20 g) mascarpone cheese

1¼ teaspoons (7 g gelatin mass (⅜ teaspoon/1 g gelatin powder hydrated in 1¼ teaspoons/6 g water)

For the sweet tart shell

See page 342

For the hazelnut crisp

See page 337

For the hazelnut praline

1⅜ cups (190 g) hazelnuts

⅓ cup (60 g) superfine (caster) sugar

1 teaspoon (4 g) fleur de sel

For the hazelnut dacquoise

2 extra-large (UK large/80 g) egg whites

3 tablespoons (35 g) superfine (caster) sugar

⅞ cup (70 g) ground hazelnuts

2 tablespoons (15 g) all-purpose (plain) flour

⅓ cup plus 2 tablespoons (55 g) confectioners' (icing) sugar

For assembly

½ cup (100 g) gianduja

¾ cup (100 g) roasted hazelnuts, lightly crushed

For the glaze

⅓ cup (100 g) neutral glaze

FOR THE HAZELNUT GANACHE

The previous day, heat the cream with the hazelnut paste in a saucepan. Filter through a conical sieve. In a large bowl, mix the white chocolate with the mascarpone and gelatin mass. Pour in the boiling liquid. Incorporate using an immersion (stick) blender until the ganache is smooth. Refrigerate for about 12 hours.

FOR THE SWEET TART SHELL

Make the tart shell (case) as described on page 342.

FOR THE HAZELNUT CRISP

Make the hazelnut crisp as described on page 337.

FOR THE HAZELNUT PRALINE

Preheat the oven to 325°F (165°C/Gas Mark 3). Roast the hazelnuts for 15 minutes. Make a dry caramel with the superfine sugar. Let cool, then process using an immersion (stick) blender. Grind the hazelnuts. In a stand mixer fitted with a flat beater attachment, mix the ground hazelnuts, caramel, and salt until well incorporated.

FOR THE HAZELNUT DACQUOISE

Make a French meringue by beating the egg whites until stiff, incorporating the superfine sugar in three batches. The meringue is ready when it forms a peak on the end of the whisk without collapsing. Fold in the ground hazelnuts, flour, and confectioners' sugar. Pipe the dacquoise batter into an 8-inch (20-cm)-diameter pastry ring. Bake for 16 minutes.

FOR ASSEMBLY

Pipe coarse lines of gianduja over the bottom of the tart shell, then sprinkle the tart shell with lightly crushed roasted hazelnuts, covering the tart shell completely. Spread a thin layer of crisp in a ring around the edge of the tart reaching halfway up the sides. Fill the center with hazelnut praline. Lift off the pastry ring from the dacquoise and trim its diameter by ⅜-¾ inch (1-2 cm) to make piping easier. Insert the dacquoise disk, leaving it flush with the top edge of the tart shell. If necessary, add more praline to make the surface smooth and flush.

FOR FINISHING

Whip the ganache with a hand mixer. Place the cake on a turntable. Use a pastry (piping) bag fitted with a size 104 Saint-Honoré tip (nozzle) to pipe the ganache in a single attempt with the turntable in motion. Hold the pastry bag in your hand at a slight angle and start piping by forming an irregular three-pointed star at the center, then continue piping in a spiral without stopping. There should be gaps in the ganache, the aim being to create a harmonious but irregular effect. For the last two or three turns, pipe a straight and even line, without irregular spurts.

FOR THE GLAZE

In a saucepan, bring the neutral topping to a boil, then transfer it to a spray gun and apply it directly to the tart.

CUSTARD TART

For the flaky brioche

⅓ cup plus 1½ tablespoons (100 g) milk

¾ small cake (13 g) fresh yeast, or 2¼ teaspoons active (easy-blend) dry yeast (dissolved in milk or water)

2 cups (285 g) bread (strong) flour

⅝ teaspoon (4 g) salt

1½ tablespoons (20 g) superfine (caster) sugar

1 large (UK medium/50 g) egg

1¾ tablespoons (25 g) unsalted butter, softened

⅔ cup (150 g) unsalted dry butter (84% fat content)

For the custard

1 cup (240 g) milk

1 jumbo (UK large/65 g) egg

1 teaspoon (2 g) vanilla pearls (or vanilla seeds)

1½ tablespoons (25 g) custard powder

¼ cup (45 g) superfine (caster) sugar

1¾ tablespoons (25 g) unsalted butter

1 pinch fleur de sel

FOR THE FLAKY BRIOCHE

In a stand mixer fitted with a dough hook, combine all the ingredients, except the butters, and mix on speed 1 while gradually adding the eggs. Increase to speed 2 and continue mixing until the dough pulls away from the sides. Cut the softened butter into cubes, add it to the dough, and knead until the dough is smooth. Knead until smooth. Let the dough rise at room temperature (68-77°F/20-25°C) for about 1 hour. Use your palms to flatten and deflate the dough, then roll it out into a rectangle. Shape the dry butter into a rectangle half the size and place it in the center of the dough. Fold over the sides of the dough to encase the butter and roll out, then fold with a simple turn (letter fold). Roll out the dough again, then fold with a double turn (book fold). Roll it out again and finish by folding with a simple turn. Roll out the dough and use it to line a 6-inch (15-cm)-diameter flower-shape tart mold previously lined with parchment (baking) paper. Freeze for about 2 hours.

FOR THE CUSTARD

In a saucepan, bring the milk to a boil. In the meantime, using a whisk, beat the eggs with the vanilla, custard powder, and sugar until thick and pale. Add the boiling milk. Return the mixture to the pan and bring back to a boil. Incorporate the butter and salt. Pour the custard over the flaky brioche dough inside the mold. Refrigerate for about 1 hour, then bake at 340°F (170°C/Gas Mark 3½) for 25 minutes.

SAINT–HONORÉ

For the flaky brioche
●

See page 335

For the choux puffs
●

See page 341

For the vanilla pastry cream
●

See page 336

For the Saint-Honoré caramel
●

1½ tablespoons (20 g) superfine
(caster) sugar

⅛ ounce (5 g) dry nougat

1 teaspoon (5 g) glucose powder

⅗ cup (170 g) isomalt

For the vanilla Chantilly cream
●

See page 335

FOR THE FLAKY BRIOCHE

Make the flaky brioche tart shell (case) as described on page 335.

FOR THE CHOUX PUFFS

Make the choux puffs as described on page 341.

FOR THE VANILLA PASTRY CREAM

Make the vanilla pastry cream as described on page 336.

FOR THE SAINT-HONORÉ CARAMEL

Mix the sugar with the dry nougat. Combine in a saucepan with 2 teaspoons (10 g) water and the glucose and place over the heat. Heat the isomalt separately. When isomalt reaches 300°F (150°C), incorporate it into the sugar and nougat mixture and cook to a dark caramel. Insert a toothpick (cocktail stick) into each choux puff and dip the rounded sides into the hot caramel. Let cool, caramel-side up, on a piece of parchment.

FOR THE VANILLA CHANTILLY CREAM

Make the vanilla Chantilly cream as described on page 335.

FOR ASSEMBLY

Fill the flaky brioche tart shell (case) with pastry cream and smooth until perfectly level. Fill the choux puffs with pastry cream. Arrange them on their sides in a ring around the edge of the brioche with the caramel-dipped side facing outward. Place six to seven choux puffs in the middle of the ring. Set aside the most perfectly formed one for decoration.

FOR FINISHING

Use a pastry (piping) bag fitted with a size 104 St. Honoré tip (nozzle) to pipe Chantilly cream petals. Starting from the center of the cake, pipe a straight line. When you reach the end of the petal, form a semicircle the size of the tip of your index finger and return to the starting point. Repeat the process over the whole tart. After completing the first ring, make three more by starting at the base of the previous petals and piping increasingly smaller petals each time. Finish by positioning a choux puff in the center as the heart of the flower.

FiG

For the diamond shortbread tart shell

●

See page 342

For the almond cream

●

See page 336

For the semi-cooked figs

●

15 (750 g) fresh figs

⅜ cup (75 g) superfine (caster) sugar

⅔ cup (150 g) fig juice

For the vanilla glaze

●

See page 341

For assembly

●

20 fresh figs

FOR THE DIAMOND SHORTBREAD TART SHELL

Make the tart shell (case) as described on page 342.

FOR THE ALMOND CREAM

Make the almond cream as described on page 336.

FOR THE SEMI-COOKED FIGS

Cut the figs into cubes and cook for a few minutes with the sugar, gradually adding the fig juice.

FOR THE VANILLA GLAZE

Make the vanilla glaze as described on page 341.

FOR ASSEMBLY

Preheat the oven to 340°F (170°C/Gas Mark 3 1/2). Fill the tart shell with almond cream. Bake for 8 minutes. Let cool for about 15 minutes, then fill halfway with semi-cooked figs. Make an attractive arrangement with thinly cut wedges of fresh fig, flesh side up, starting from the edges and working your way toward the center. Brush with vanilla glaze.

PEACH

For the sweet tart shell

See page 342

For the vanilla pastry cream

¾ cup (185 g) milk

2 tablespoons (30 g) whipping cream

1 vanilla bean (pod)

1 extra-large (UK large/60 g) egg

¼ cup (50 g) superfine (caster) sugar

1 tablespoon (16 g) custard powder

1½ tablespoons (20 g) unsalted butter, softened

3 tablespoons (40 g) mascarpone cheese

For the almond and vanilla cream

See page 336

For the peach and verbena gel

3½ tablespoons (40 g) superfine (caster) sugar

1⅛ teaspoons (5 g) agar powder

1¾ cups (400 g) peach puree

5 fresh verbena leaves, chopped

1 teaspoon (2 g) verbena peppercorns, coarsely ground

For assembly

5 white peaches

5 yellow peaches

⅓ cup (50 g) nectarine

⅓ cup (50 g) red peach

⅓ cup (50 g) white peach

⅓ cup (100 g) neutral glaze

½ teaspoon (1 g) vanilla pearls (or vanilla seeds)

FOR THE SWEET TART SHELL

Make the sweet tart shell (case) as described on page 342.

FOR THE VANILLA PASTRY CREAM

Make the vanilla pastry cream as described on page 336.

FOR THE ALMOND AND VANILLA CREAM

Make the almond and vanilla cream as described on page 336.

FOR THE PEACH AND VERBENA GEL

Mix together the sugar and agar powder. In a saucepan, bring the peach puree to a boil. Add the sugar and agar powder and incorporate using an immersion (stick) blender. Let cool. When the gel is cold, mix with an immersion blender, being careful not to beat in any air. Add the chopped verbena leaves and verbena pepper. Mix everything together gently.

FOR ASSEMBLY

Preheat the oven to 340°F (170°C/Gas Mark 3 1/2). Fill the tart shell with almond and vanilla cream and bake for 8 minutes. Let cool for about 15 minutes. Peel and cut the white and yellow peaches into thin wedges. Pipe a ball of pastry cream at the center of the tart to serve as a reference point. Pipe a ball of pastry cream at the edge of the tart and continue inward to make a strip reaching the ball at the center. Repeat the process with the peach and verbena gel. Cover the entire tart with alternating strips. Cut the nectarine and ⅓ cup (50 g) red and white peaches into cubes and arrange uniformly on the tart. Smooth with a spatula (palette knife). Arrange the peach wedges in a rosette pattern. In a saucepan, combine the neutral glaze with the vanilla pearls and bring to a boil. Transfer the mixture to a spray gun and flock the tart with glaze.

APRiCOT

For the flaky brioche

See page 335

For the apricot preserves

11 (385 g) apricots

3 tablespoons (45 g) apricot puree

1 drizzle olive oil

2½ tablespoons (30 g) superfine (caster) sugar

2 tablespoons plus ¾ teaspoon (30 g) glucose powder

1½ teaspoons (6 g) pectin NH

⅜ teaspoon (2 g) tartaric acid

For the savory Chantilly cream

1¾ cups (430 g) whipping cream

½ cup (20 g) fresh savory

3¾ teaspoons (15 g) superfine (caster) sugar

3 tablespoons (45 g) mascarpone cheese

2½ teaspoons (14 g) gelatin mass (¾ teaspoon/2 g gelatin powder hydrated in 2½ teaspoons/12 g water)

For the vanilla glaze

See page 341

For the caramelized apricots

7 apricots

1½ tablespoons (20 g) unsalted butter

2½ tablespoons (50 g) honey

152

FOR THE FLAKY BRIOCHE

Make the flaky brioche tart shell (case) as described on page 335.

FOR THE APRICOT PRESERVES

In a saucepan, caramelize the apricots and apricot puree with the olive oil, then simmer over low heat for about 30 minutes. Add the sugar, glucose, pectin, and tartaric acid. Mix well and bring to a boil for 1 minute. Refrigerate until set.

FOR THE SAVORY CHANTILLY CREAM

In a saucepan, combine one-third of the cream with the savory and sugar and bring to a boil. Pour the boiling mixture over the mascarpone and gelatin mass. Filter through a conical sieve and incorporate using an immersion (stick) blender, gradually adding the remaining cream. Refrigerate.

FOR THE VANILLA GLAZE

Make the vanilla glaze as described on page 341.

FOR THE CARAMELIZED APRICOTS

Halve the apricots and caramelize them in a skillet (frying pan) with the butter and honey. Transfer to a Silpat mat and coat with the vanilla glaze.

FOR FINISHING

Whip the Chantilly cream using a hand mixer. Spread a layer of apricot preserves over the flaky brioche tart shell (case), then make a small mound in the middle. Arrange the glazed caramelized apricot halves around it. Use a pastry (piping) bag fitted with a size 20 Saint-Honoré tip (nozzle) to pipe flames of Chantilly cream from the outer edge toward the center, filling in any gaps. Finish by positioning an apricot at the center.

M LON

For the melon sorbet

½ cup plus 1 tablespoon (110 g) superfine (caster) sugar

¼ cup (60 g) glucose powder

2¾ cups (650 g) fresh melon puree

4 teaspoons (20 g) lemon juice

For the meringue

3¾ large (UK medium/125 g) egg whites (½ cup)

⅔ cup (125 g) superfine (caster) sugar

1 cup (125 g) confectioners' (icing) sugar

For the vanilla Chantilly cream

See page 335

For the melon

2 melons

FOR THE MELON SORBET

Mix together the superfine sugar and glucose. In a saucepan, heat ½ cup plus 1 tablespoon (140 g) water and add the sugar and glucose mixture. Bring to a boil, then pour the mixture over the melon puree and lemon juice. Incorporate using an immersion (stick) blender, then churn in an ice cream maker. Set aside in the freezer.

FOR THE MERINGUE

Preheat the oven to 200°F (90°C). Beat the egg whites until stiff, adding the superfine sugar in three batches. The meringue is ready when it forms a peak on the end of the whisk without collapsing. Sift the confectioners' sugar. On a baking sheet lined with a Silpat mat, pipe the meringue over the outside of a flower-shape baking pan. Bake for 1 hour to 1 hour 30 minutes. Let cool, then carefully remove the baking pan. Turn the meringue over to form a tart shell (case).

FOR THE VANILLA CHANTILLY CREAM

Make the vanilla Chantilly cream as described on page 335.

FOR THE MELON

Use a cookie cutter to cut out teardrop-shape pieces of melon.

FOR ASSEMBLY

Whip the Chantilly cream with a hand mixer. Fill the meringue shell with a ⅜- inch (1-cm)-thick layer of sorbet. Use a pastry bag fitted with a ⅜-inch (10-mm) plain tip to pipe small balls of Chantilly cream over the top. Start from the outside of the tart and work your way to the middle. Make an attractive arrangement with the melon teardrops, starting with a ring in the center.

FALL

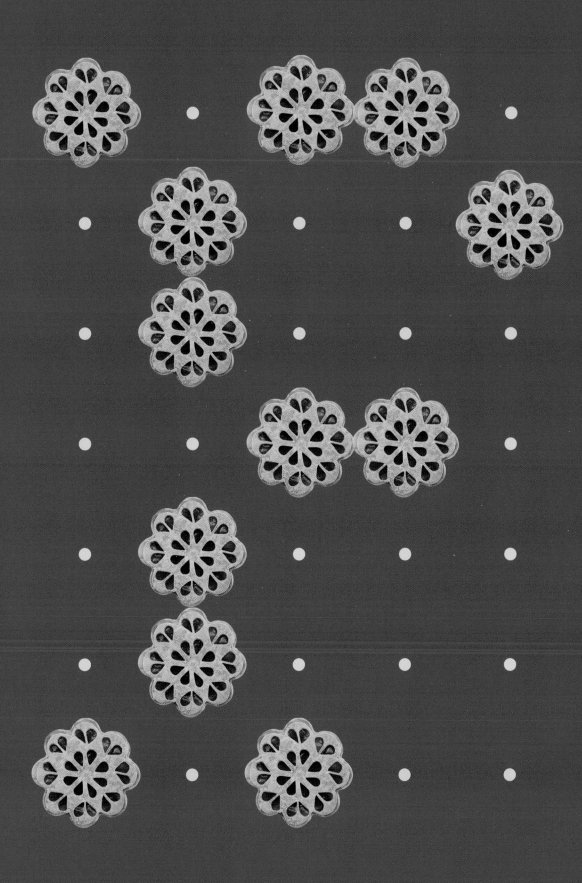

YUZU

For the yuzu ganache

3⅓ cups (800 g) whipping cream

2½ tablespoons (42 g) gelatin mass
(1⅛ teaspoons/6 g gelatin powder
hydrated in 2½ tablespoons/36 g
water)

7½ ounces (215 g) white couverture
chocolate, chopped

¾ cup (180 g) yuzu juice

For the reconstituted Breton
shortbread

See page 343

For the pain de Gênes cake

See page 335

For the lemon marmalade insert

2½ tablespoons (30 g) superfine
(caster) sugar

1⅞ teaspoons (5 g) agar powder

1¼ cups (300 g) lemon juice

⅜ teaspoon (1 g) xanthan gum

⅓ cup (15 g) fresh mint leaves,
chopped

4-5 (55 g) finger lime caviar
(pearls)

1 cup (170 g) candied lemon peel,
finely chopped

3 tablespoons (40 g) lemon suprêmes

For the yellow chocolate coating

See page 338

For the gold glitter

scant 1 cup (220 g) kirsch

1½ cups (120 g) gold luster dust

161

FOR THE YUZU GANACHE

The previous day, heat half of the cream in a saucepan and add the gelatin mass. Gradually pour the mixture over the chopped chocolate. Whisk until smooth. Use an immersion (stick) blender to incorporate the remaining cream, followed by the yuzu juice. Blend until smooth and refrigerate for about 12 hours.

FOR THE RECONSTITUTED BRETON SHORTBREAD

Make the reconstituted Breton shortbread as described on page 343.

FOR THE PAIN DE GÊNES CAKE

Make the pain de Gênes cake as described on page 335.

FOR THE LEMON MARMALADE INSERT

Mix together the sugar and agar. In a saucepan, bring the lemon juice to a boil, then add the sugar and agar mixture. Let cool. When cold, mix with an immersion blender, being careful not to beat in any air. Add the xanthan gum. Mix the gel with the chopped mint leaves, finger lime caviar, finely diced candied lemon peel, and the suprêmes, coarsely cut into small pieces. Pour the mixture into a 6¼-inch (16-cm)-diameter mold and freeze for about 3 hours, until set.

FOR THE YELLOW CHOCOLATE COATING

Make the yellow chocolate coating as described on page 338.

FOR THE GOLD GLITTER

Mix the kirsch with the gold luster dust.

FOR ASSEMBLY

Whip the ganache with a hand mixer. Trim the reconstituted Breton shortbread disk to the same size as the pain de Gênes disk. Lay the pain de Gênes disk on top of the other. Place the lemon marmalade insert on top. Freeze for about 6 hours. Pipe ganache over the entire surface of a 7-inch (18-cm)-diameter Pavoni silicone entremets mold. Pipe more in the middle so the insert will be well centered. Add the insert and cover with ganache. Smooth with a spatula (palette knife). Freeze for about 6 hours, until set. Carefully unmold.

FOR FINISHING

Step 1
Using a No. 125 St. Honoré tip (nozzle), start by piping ganache around the outside of the entremets. Hold the pastry (piping) bag horizontally and pipe large petals, working from the bottom to the top. Stop when you reach the top, leaving space in which to pipe the central flower.

Step 2
Using the same nozzle, but this time holding the pastry bag vertically, pipe the central flower of the entremets. Pipe a dot of ganache at the center—it will be your reference point—then pipe irregular lines from the outside toward the middle (almost reaching the centered dot).

Step 3
Using a pastry bag fitted with a $^1/_{16}$-inch (1-mm) plain tip, pipe small peaks of ganache at the center to form the pistils of the flower. Use a spray gun to uniformly flock the entremets with yellow chocolate coating. Repeat the process with the gold glitter. Refrigerate for about 4 hours before serving.

PARIS-BREST

For the hazelnut praline
●
See page 342

For the vanilla pastry cream
●
See page 336

For the Paris-Brest cream
●
1¼ cups (300 g) vanilla pastry cream

⅔ cup (200 g) hazelnut praline

7 tablespoons (100 g) unsalted butter, softened

⅔ cup (140 g) mascarpone cheese

3¾ teaspoons (21 g) gelatin mass (1 teaspoon/3 g gelatin powder hydrated in 3¾ teaspoons/18 g water)

For the sweet tart shell
●
See page 342

For the hazelnut crisp
●
See page 337

For the choux puffs
●
See page 341

For assembly
●
2 cups (250 g) gianduja

For the vanilla glaze
●
⅓ cup (100 g) neutral glaze
½ teaspoon (1 g) vanilla pearls (or vanilla seeds)

FOR THE HAZELNUT PRALINE

Make the hazelnut praline as described on page 342.

FOR THE VANILLA PASTRY CREAM

Make the vanilla pastry cream as described on page 336.

FOR THE PARIS-BREST CREAM

Reheat the vanilla pastry cream, if necessary. Add the hazelnut praline, butter, mascarpone, and gelatin mass to the hot pastry cream. Incorporate using an immersion (stick) blender. Refrigerate for about 12 hours.

FOR THE SWEET TART SHELL

Make the sweet tart shell (case) as described on page 342.

FOR THE HAZELNUT CRISP

Make the hazelnut crisp as described on page 337.

FOR THE CHOUX PUFFS

Make the choux puffs as described on page 341.

FOR ASSEMBLY

Fill the tart shell to three-quarters with the crisp. Fill half of the choux puffs with 1 cup (240 g) of the gianduja and the remaining puffs with the hazelnut praline. Arrange the choux evenly in a ring, alternating the flavors. Set aside the most perfectly formed, hazelnut praline-filled choux puff for the center when decorating. Smooth the surface of the Paris-Brest cream to fill in any gaps. Position the reserved choux puff in the center and cover with the remaining 2½ teaspoons (10 g) melted gianduja.

166

FOR FINISHING

Whip the Paris-Brest cream with a hand mixer. Using a metal stand and a pastry (piping) bag fitted with a size 125 Saint-Honoré tip (nozzle), and starting from the center, pipe irregular petals with the cream to create a pretty flower. Pipe in a circular motion from left to right to make ¾-inch (2-cm) semicircular petals in the middle, then gradually increase the size of the semicircles and start each petal in the middle of the preceding one.

FOR THE VANILLA GLAZE

In a saucepan, combine the neutral glaze with the vanilla pearls and bring to a boil. Transfer the mixture to a spray gun and flock the tart with glaze.

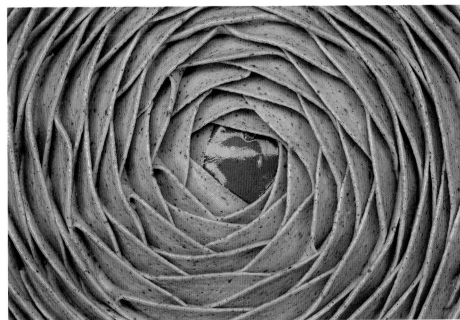

BLACK  ORΣST

For the kirsch ganache

1⅞ cups (440 g) whipping cream

3½ ounces (100 g) white chocolate, chopped

1½ tablespoons (25 g) gelatin mass (1 teaspoon/3.5 g gelatin powder hydrated in 1½ tablespoons/21.5 g water)

2 tablespoons (30 g) kirsch

For the flourless chocolate cake

8 large (UK medium/135 g) egg yolks

1 cup plus 1 tablespoon (210 g) superfine (caster) sugar

5¾ large (UK medium/190 g) egg whites (¾ cup)

⅔ cup (60 g) unsweetened cocoa powder

For the chocolate and fleur de sel shortbread

See page 343

For the dark chocolate coating

¼ cup (50 g) cocoa butter

1¾ ounces (50 g) bittersweet (dark) chocolate (70% cocoa), chopped

For the chocolate crisp

1¾ ounces (50 g) dark chocolate coating

8½ ounces (240 g) chocolate and fleur de sel shortbread

For the morello cherry gel

2 cups (500 g) morello cherry puree

2¼ teaspoons (6 g) xanthan gum

5⅓ cup cups (750 g) pitted morello cherries

½ cup (125 g) morello cherries in kirsch

For the charcoal black chocolate coating

See page 338

168

FOR THE KIRSCH GANACHE

The previous day, bring half the cream to a boil in a saucepan. Pour the hot cream over the chopped chocolate and gelatin mass. Incorporate using an immersion (stick) blender, adding the remaining cream and the kirsch, until the ganache is smooth. Filter through a conical sieve and refrigerate for about 12 hours.

FOR THE FLOURLESS CHOCOLATE CAKE

Preheat the oven to 350°F (175°C/Gas Mark 4). Beat the yolks with half the sugar. Beat the egg whites until stiff with the other half. Combine the two, mix, and add the cocoa. Transfer the batter to a 1¼-inch (3-cm)-deep, straight-sided baking pan and bake for 20 minutes. After taking the cake out of the oven, use a 6¼-inch (16-cm)-diameter pastry ring to cut the cake into a disk. Then use a 5½-inch (14-cm)-diameter pastry ring to cut out the center.

FOR THE CHOCOLATE AND FLEUR DE SEL SHORTBREAD

Make the chocolate and fleur de sel shortbread as described on page 343.

FOR THE DARK CHOCOLATE COATING

Melt and pour the cocoa butter over the chopped chocolate. Incorporate using an immersion blender until smooth.

FOR THE CHOCOLATE CRISP

Mix the dark chocolate coating with the chocolate and fleur de sel shortbread. Position a 5½-inch (14-cm)-diameter pastry ring inside a 6¼-inch (16-cm)-diameter one and fill in the space between them with crisp to make a ring.

FOR THE MORELLO CHERRY GEL

Blend the puree with the xanthan gum. Add the cherries. Pour the resulting gel over the chocolate cake ring to make the insert. Freeze for about 6 hours, until set.

FOR THE CHARCOAL BLACK CHOCOLATE COATING

Make the charcoal black coating as described on page 338.

FOR ASSEMBLY

Complete the insert by placing the ring of cake and gel over the ring of crisp. Add a thin layer of ganache and fill to the top with gel. Freeze for about 2 hours. Pipe the ganache over the entire surface of a 7-inch (18-cm)-diameter tube cake pan. Pipe more in the middle so the insert will be well centered. Add the insert and cover with ganache. Smooth with a spatula (palette knife). Freeze for at least 6 hours, until set, then carefully unmold the cake.

FOR FINISHING

Whip the remaining ganache with a hand mixer. Use a pastry (piping) bag fitted with a size 125 Saint-Honoré tip (nozzle) to pipe the ganache in such as way as to enhance the shape of the cake. To do this, hold the bag completely upright and pipe irregular semicircular lines. Start piping on the inside of the ring, working from the bottom and stopping at the top. Then repeat the process on the outside of the cake. Use a spray gun to uniformly flock the cake with the charcoal black chocolate coating. Refrigerate for about 4 hours before serving.

PECAN

FOR THE BASIC COMPONENTS

For the pecan cream
●

4½ tablespoons (65 g) unsalted
butter, softened
⅓ cup (65 g) superfine (caster)
sugar
¾ cup (65 g) ground pecans
1 jumbo (UK large/65 g) egg

For the pecan praline
●

See page 343

FLOWER TART,
OPÉRA VERSION

For the diamond shortbread tart
shell
●

See page 342

For the caramel sauce
●

See page 335

For the caramelized pecans
●

2 cups (200 g) pecans
¼ cup plus 1 tablespoon (60 g)
superfine (caster) sugar

scant ¼ teaspoon (1 g) tartaric
acid

SCULPTED NUT,
MEURICE VERSION

For the pecan ganache
●

2 cups (500 g) whipping cream
3 large (UK medium/50 g) egg yolks
2 tablespoons (25 g) superfine
(caster) sugar
1¾ teaspoons (10 g) gelatin mass
(½ teaspoon/1.5 g gelatin powder
hydrated in 1¾ teaspoons/8.5 g
water)
½ cup (150 g) pecan paste
5¼ ounces (150 g) pecan gel
⅞ cup (200 g) mascarpone cheese

For the sweet tart shell
●

See page 342

For the pecan praline
●

5 cups (500 g) pecans
⅔ cup (125 g) superfine (caster)
sugar
2½ teaspoons (10 g) fleur de sel

For the pecan crisp
●

See page 337

For the walnut milk
●

2 cups (500 g) milk
½ cup (50 g) shelled walnuts

For the pecan gel
●

1 quantity (500 g) walnut milk
3 tablespoons (35 g) superfine
(caster) sugar
4¾ extra-large (UK large/90 g) egg
yolks (⅜ cup)
1⅞ teaspoons (5 g) xanthan gum
¼ cup (75 g) pecan paste

For the chocolate nut coating
●

1 cup (200 g) cocoa butter
1¾ ounces (50 g) milk chocolate,
chopped
5¼ ounces (150 g) white chocolate,
chopped
¼ teaspoon (1 g) yellow food
coloring

FOR THE PECAN CREAM

In a stand mixer fitted with a flat beater attachment, cream the butter with the superfine sugar and ground pecans. Gradually incorporate the eggs, then refrigerate.

FOR THE PECAN PRALINE

Make the pecan praline as described on page 343.

FOR THE BASIC COMPONENTS

Make the pecan cream and praline as described above.

FOR THE DIAMOND SHORTBREAD TART SHELL

Make the tart shell (case) as described on page 342.

FOR THE CARAMEL SAUCE

Make the caramel sauce as described on page 335.

FOR THE CARAMELIZED PECANS

Preheat the oven to 340°F (170°C/Gas Mark 3½). Roast the pecans for 15 minutes. In a saucepan, heat the superfine sugar, 1½ tablespoons (25 g) water, and the tartaric acid until it turns into a dark caramel. Add the pecans, tossing to coat, and let them caramelize for a few minutes, then transfer to a baking sheet lined with a Silpat mat too cool. Space the pecans apart to prevent them from sticking together. Do not turn off the oven.

FOR ASSEMBLY

Spread the pecan cream over the bottom of the tart shell and bake at 340°F (170°C/Gas Mark 3½) for 8 minutes. Cover with a layer of caramel sauce. Pipe dots of pecan praline. Arrange the caramelized pecans in a rosette pattern.

FOR THE PECAN GANACHE

In a saucepan, bring the cream to a boil. Beat the yolks with the superfine sugar. Pour a little boiling cream over this mixture, then return it to the saucepan to make a crème anglaise and cook for 2 minutes. Incorporate the gelatin mass, pecan paste, and pecan gel using an immersion (stick) blender. Filter through a conical sieve and add the mascarpone. Refrigerate for about 12 hours.

FOR THE BASIC COMPONENTS

Make the pecan cream and praline, as described on page 175.

FOR THE SWEET TART SHELL

In a stand mixer fitted with a flat beater, cream the butter with the confectioners' sugar, ground hazelnuts, and salt. Add and beat in the eggs, then add the flour and starch. Mix until smooth. Refrigerate for 4 hours. Preheat the oven to 325°F (165°C/Gas Mark 3). Roll out the dough to a ⅛-inch (3-mm) thickness and line 3¼-4-inch (8-10-cm)-long oval (calisson-shape) silicone molds with the dough. Trim off the excess with a knife. Prick the tart shells (bases) with a fork. Bake for 25 minutes.

FOR THE PECAN PRALINE

Make the pecan praline as described on page 343.

FOR THE PECAN CRISP

Make the pecan crisp as described on page 337.

FOR THE WALNUT MILK

Process the milk and walnuts in a juicer.

FOR THE PECAN GEL

In a saucepan, heat the walnut milk to just before boiling. Using a whisk, beat the egg yolks with the superfine sugar until thick and pale. Add part of the hot walnut milk and let cook for 1-2 minutes. Let cool. Incorporate using the immersion blender and add the xanthan gum and walnut paste. Filter through a conical sieve and refrigerate until set.

FOR THE CHOCOLATE NUT COATING

In a saucepan, melt the cocoa butter, then pour it over the chopped chocolates. Add the food coloring and blend until smooth.

ASSEMBLING THE SCULPTED PECANS

Preheat the oven to 340°F (170°C/Gas Mark 3½). Spread the pecan cream inside the tart shells and bake for 8 minutes. Fill to the top with pecan crisp. Smooth with a spatula (palette knife). Fill other, slightly smaller oval (calisson-shape) silicone molds with the pecan gel. Freeze until set, then place the inserts on top of the tarts.

FOR FINISHING

Whip the ganache with a hand mixer. Use a pastry (piping) bag fitted with a ¼-inch (6-mm) plain tip (nozzle) to pipe coarse and irregular lines of ganache over the inserts to resemble nutshells. Start at one end and work your way to the other. Insert toothpicks (cocktail sticks) into the frozen inserts and dip them in the chocolate nut coating at 86°F (30°C). Dip a makeup brush in the cocoa powder and lightly tap the cocoa on certain parts of the sculpted pecans. Rub with a cloth to remove the excess and create the effect of shading. Remove the toothpicks and set the inserts on the tarts.

For the pistachio ganache

See page 340

For the pistachio praline

See page 343

For the pistachio milk
●
See page 341

For the pistachio gel

See page 341

For the pistachio crisp

See page 337

For the green chocolate coating
●
See page 338

For the pistachio dacquoise

2½ large (UK medium/80 g) egg whites (⅓ cup)

3 tablespoons (35 g) superfine (caster) sugar

¾ cup (70 g) ground almonds

2 tablespoons (15 g) all-purpose (plain) flour

⅓ cup plus 2 tablespoons (55 g) confectioners' (icing) sugar

FOR THE PISTACHIO GANACHE

Make the pistachio ganache as described on page 340.

FOR THE PISTACHIO PRALINE

Make the pistachio praline as described on page 343.

FOR THE PISTACHIO MILK

Make the pistachio milk as described on page 341.

FOR THE PISTACHIO GEL

Make the pistachio gel as described on page 341.

FOR THE PISTACHIO CRISP

Make the pistachio crisp as described on page 337.

FOR THE PISTACHIO DACQUOISE

Preheat the oven to 340°F (170°C/Gas Mark 3½). Make a French meringue by beating the egg whites until stiff, incorporating the superfine sugar in three batches. The meringue is ready when it forms a peak on the end of the whisk without collapsing. Fold in the ground almonds, flour, and confectioners' sugar. Pipe the dacquoise batter into a 6¼-inch (16-cm)-diameter pastry ring and bake for 16 minutes.

FOR THE GREEN CHOCOLATE COATING

Make the green chocolate coating as described on page 338.

FOR ASSEMBLY

Whip the ganache with a hand mixer. Carefully lift off the pastry ring from the crisp. Replace it with another pastry ring of the same size lined with an acetate strip. Place the dacquoise disk on top. Cover with a thin layer of praline, then with a layer of pistachio gel. Freeze for about 3 hours. Pipe ganache over the entire surface of a 7-inch (18-cm)-diameter Pavoni silicone entremets mold. Pipe more in the middle so the insert will be well centered. Introduce the insert, cover with ganache, and smooth with a spatula (palette knife). Freeze for about 6 hours, until set, before carefully unmolding.

FOR FINISHING

Use a pastry (piping) bag fitted with a size 104 Saint-Honoré tip (nozzle) to pipe the ganache. Start from the edge of the entremets and pipe ¾-1⅛-inch (2-3-cm)-wide waves to the center. Place in the freezer, then use a 2½-inch (6-cm)-diameter cookie cutter to make a hole in the center. Use a spray gun to uniformly flock the entremets with the green chocolate coating. Fill the center with the remaining praline. Refrigerate for about 4 hours before serving.

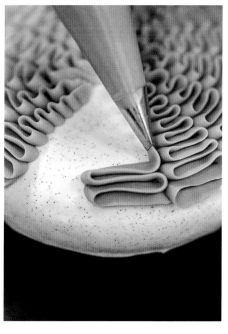

CHESTNUT AND BLACK CURRANT

For the chestnut mixture

●

¼ cup (80 g) sweetened condensed milk

1 cup (200 g) crème de marrons (chestnut spread)

1 cup (200 g) chestnut paste

For the sweet tart shell

●

See page 342

For the black currant preserves

●

3½ cups (385 g) black currants

3 tablespoons (45 g) black currant puree

1 drizzle olive oil

2½ tablespoons (30 g) superfine (caster) sugar

2 tablespoons plus ¾ teaspoon (30 g) glucose powder

1½ teaspoons (6 g) pectin NH

⅜ teaspoon (2 g) tartaric acid

For the vanilla Chantilly cream

●

See page 335

For the almond cream

●

See page 336

For the orange chocolate coating

●

See page 338

For assembly

●

10 (100 g) candied chestnuts

For finishing

●

1 candied chestnut

184

FOR THE CHESTNUT MIXTURE

In a copper saucepan, caramelize the condensed milk in the oven at 195°F (90°C) for 4 hours. Let cool, then transfer to a food processor. Add the chestnut paste and spread plus 2 tablespoons plus 2 teaspoons (40 g) water and blend until the mixture thickens. Refrigerate for about 12 hours.

FOR THE SWEET TART SHELL

Make the sweet tart shell (case) as described on page 342.

FOR THE BLACK CURRANT PRESERVES

In a saucepan, caramelize the black currants and black currant puree with the olive oil, then simmer over low heat for about 30 minutes. Add the sugar, glucose, pectin, and tartaric acid. Mix well and bring to a boil for 1 minute. Refrigerate until set.

FOR THE VANILLA CHANTILLY CREAM

Make the vanilla Chantilly cream as described on page 335.

FOR THE ALMOND CREAM

Make the almond cream as described on page 336.

FOR THE ORANGE CHOCOLATE COATING

Make the orange chocolate coating as described on page 338.

FOR ASSEMBLY

Preheat the oven to 340°F (170°C/Gas Mark 3½). Spread a thin layer of almond and vanilla cream inside the tart shell. Bake for 8 minutes and let cool for about 15 minutes. Pipe dots of the black currant preserves and the chestnut mixture all over the surface of the tart. Break up the caramelized chestnut mixture into pieces and add. Fill any gaps with Chantilly cream and smooth with a spatula (palette knife) to create an even surface. Freeze for about 6 hours.

FOR FINISHING

Use a pastry (piping) bag fitted with a small star tip (nozzle) to pipe the Chantilly cream in small waves from top to bottom. Use a spray gun to uniformly flock the entremets with the orange chocolate coating. Decorate the center with the candied chestnut.

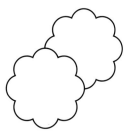

MATCHA

For the tea ganache

3¼ cups (780 g) whipping cream

½ cup (50 g) green matcha tea powder

6¼ ounces (175 g) white couverture chocolate, chopped

2½ tablespoons (42 g) gelatin mass (2 teaspoons/7 g gelatin powder hydrated in 2 tablespoons plus 1¼ teaspoons/35 g water)

For the almond and timut pepper crisp

See page 337

For the Japanese matcha cake

2 tablespoons plus 2 teaspoons (40 g) milk

scant ¼ teaspoon (1 g) salt

¼ cup (45 g) superfine (caster) sugar

2½ tablespoons (15 g) green matcha tea powder

1½ tablespoons (20 g) unsalted butter

¼ cup plus 1½ teaspoons (35 g) cake (Italian "00") flour

2 small (75 g) eggs

1 tablespoon plus 2 teaspoons (25 g) grapeseed oil

2¼ large (UK medium/75 g) egg whites (⅓ cup)

¼ cup (40 g) fresh strawberry slices

For the matcha crémeux

2 cups (500 g) milk

5¼ large (UK medium/90 g) egg yolks (⅜ cup)

3 tablespoons (35 g) superfine (caster) sugar

1 teaspoon (2.5 g) xanthan gum

¼ cup (25 g) green matcha tea powder

For the matcha gel

1⅛ cups (275 g) lemon juice

2½ tablespoons (15 g) green matcha tea powder

1½ tablespoons (20 g) superfine (caster) sugar

1⅛ teaspoons (3 g) agar powder

⅜ teaspoon (1 g) xanthan gum

For the green chocolate coating

See page 338

189

FOR THE TEA GANACHE

The previous day, heat half of the cream in a saucepan. Add the matcha, remove from the heat, cover, and let infuse for about 10 minutes. Heat the mixture again and filter through a conical sieve. Pour it over the chopped chocolate and gelatin mass, then add the remaining cream. Incorporate using an immersion (stick) blender until the ganache is smooth. Refrigerate for about 12 hours.

FOR THE ALMOND AND TIMUT PEPPER CRISP

Make the almond and timut pepper crisp as described on page 337.

FOR THE JAPANESE MATCHA CAKE

Preheat the oven to 325°F (165°C/Gas Mark 3). In a saucepan, combine the milk with 2 tablespoons plus 2 teaspoons (40 g) water, the salt, ½ teaspoon (2.5 g) of the sugar, the matcha tea, and butter and bring to a boil. Let boil for 1-2 minutes, then add the flour and stir over low heat until the paste pulls away easily from the sides of the pan. Transfer to a stand mixer fitted with a flat beater attachment. Mix to release the steam, then gradually add the eggs and oil. Beat the egg whites until stiff, adding the remaining sugar in three stages. The meringue is ready when it forms a peak on the end of the whisk without collapsing. Fold into the batter in three batches until incorporated and smooth. Pipe into a 6¼-inch (16-cm)-diameter pastry ring to a thickness of about ⅜ inch (1 cm). Insert the strawberry slices into the batter. Bake for about 1 hour. Let cool.

FOR THE MATCHA CRÉMEUX

In a saucepan, heat the milk to just before boiling. Using a whisk, beat the egg yolks with the sugar until thick and pale. Add part of the hot milk and cook for 1-2 minutes. Let cool, then incorporate using an immersion (stick) blender, adding the xanthan gum and matcha. Filter through a conical sieve and refrigerate.

FOR THE MATCHA GEL

In a saucepan, bring the lemon juice to a boil. Add the matcha and let boil for 5 minutes, then incorporate the sugar, agar, and xanthan gum using an immersion blender and refrigerate until set. Blend again.

FOR THE GREEN CHOCOLATE COATING

Make the green chocolate coating as described on page 338.

FOR ASSEMBLY

Whip the ganache with a hand mixer. Carefully lift off the pastry ring from the cake. Replace it with another pastry ring of the same size lined with an acetate strip and spread a thin layer of crisp inside. Place the cake disk on top. Add a layer of crémeux, followed by a layer of gel, smoothing to make them as even as possible. Freeze for about 6 hours. Pipe ganache over the entire surface of a 7-inch (18-cm)-diameter Pavoni silicone entremets mold. Pipe more in the middle so the insert will be well centered. Add the insert and cover with ganache. Smooth with a spatula (palette knife). Freeze for about 6 hours, until set.

FOR FiNiSHiNG

Use a pastry (piping) bag fitted with a size 125 tip (nozzle) to pipe the remaining ganache over the entire surface of the cake. With a continuous back-and-forth motion, pipe loops of intertwined ribbons, as if the ganache has "come to life." Use a spray gun to uniformly flock the entremets with the green chocolate coating.

APPL

For the sweet tart shell
●
See page 342

For the almond cream
●
See page 336

For the apple compote
●
6-7 Granny Smith apples (1 kg)
½ cup (125 g) lemon juice

For assembly
●
1 Granny Smith apple, cubed
10 Royal Gala apples

FOR THE SWEET TART SHELL

Make the tart shell (case) as described on page 342.

FOR THE ALMOND CREAM

Make the almond cream as described on page 336.

FOR THE APPLE COMPOTE

Peel and chop the apples into small cubes. In a saucepan, combine the chopped apples with the lemon juice. Cook gently until the apples are stewed.

FOR ASSEMBLY

Preheat the oven to 340°F (170°C/Gas Mark 3½). Fill the tart shell halfway with almond cream. Distribute the Granny Smith apple cubes evenly over the cream and press lightly with your fingers. Bake for about 8 minutes. Then let cool for about 15 minutes. Fill to three-quarters with the apple compote. Rinse the Royal Gala apples and cut, unpeeled, into thin slices with a mandoline. Arrange the slices upright in a staggered pattern, starting at the edge of the tart and working toward the center. To make the center, make a line with five apple slices in a brickwork pattern and roll it up. Insert into the middle of the tart.

For the sweet tartlet shells

½ cup (1 stick/115 g) unsalted butter

½ cup plus 1 tablespoon (70 g) confectioners' (icing) sugar

¼ cup (25 g) ground hazelnuts

scant ¼ teaspoon (1 g) salt

1 medium (UK small/45 g) egg

1⅜ cups (190 g) bread (strong) flour

⅜ cup (60 g) potato starch

For the almond cream

See page 336

For the quince teardrops

8 quinces

1 cup (200 g) superfine (caster) sugar

¾ cup (200 g) lemon juice

¼ cup (70 g) yuzu juice

For the quince preserves

1 pound (500 g) quince scraps (trimmings, from 5½ quinces)

⅓ cup (100 g) quince cooking syrup

For the vanilla glaze

See page 341

FOR THE SWEET TART SHELL

Preheat the oven to 325°F (165°C/Gas Mark 3). In a stand mixer fitted with a flat beater, cream the butter with the confectioners' sugar, ground hazelnuts, and salt. Add and beat with the egg, then add the flour and starch. Mix until smooth. Roll out the dough to an ⅛-inch (3-mm) thickness and line 3¼-inch (8-cm)-diameter flower-shape tartlet molds with the dough. Trim off the excess with a knife. Prick the tartlet shells (cases) with a fork. Bake for 25 minutes.

FOR THE ALMOND CREAM

Make the almond cream as described on page 336.

FOR THE QUINCE TEARDROPS

Wash and peel the quinces. Separate and reserve 7 ounces (200 g) peels from 2¼ quinces for making the syrup and the remaining 1 pound 2 ounces (500 g) quince peels from 5¾ quinces for making the preserves. Use a cookie cutter to cut two-thirds of the quince pieces into teardrops, making about 10½ ounces (300 g). In a saucepan combine the reserved peels for the syrup with 4¼ cups (1 kg) water, the superfine sugar, lemon juice, and yuzu juice. Reduce to a pink syrup. Add the quince teardrops and let poach for about 20 minutes. Set aside the cooking syrup.

FOR THE QUINCE PRESERVES

Cook the remaining reserved quince peels in the cooking syrup. The preserves are ready when the individual pieces cannot be discerned.

FOR THE VANILLA GLAZE

Make the vanilla glaze as described on page 341.

FOR ASSEMBLY

Preheat the oven to 340°F (170°C/Gas Mark 3½). Fill the tartlet shells with almond and vanilla cream. Bake for 8 minutes. Let cool for about 15 minutes, then fill halfway with quince preserves. Arrange the quince teardrops in a flower on top, then brush with the vanilla glaze.

APPLE

PRESSÉ

For the flaky brioche

½ cup (125 g) milk

⅞ small cake (15 g) fresh yeast, or 2⅝ teaspoons active dry (easy-blend) yeast, dissolved in milk or water

2½ cups (340 g) bread (strong) flour

scant 1 teaspoon (5 g) salt

1½ tablespoons (20 g) superfine (caster) sugar

1 jumbo (UK large/60 g) egg

2 tablespoons (30 g) unsalted butter, softened

¾ cup plus 1 tablespoon (180 g) unsalted dry butter (84% fat content)

For the apple pressé

20 apples

For the caramel sauce

See page 33

FOR THE FLAKY BRIOCHE

In a stand mixer fitted with a dough hook, combine the milk, yeast, flour, salt, and sugar and mix on speed 1 while gradually adding the egg. Increase to speed 2 and continue mixing until the dough pulls away from the sides. Cut the softened butter into cubes and knead into a smooth dough. Let the dough rise at room temperature (68-77°F/20-25°C) for about 1 hour. Use your palms to flatten and deflate the dough, then roll out into a rectangle. Shape the dry butter into a rectangle half the size and place it in the center of the dough. Fold over the sides of the dough to encase the butter and roll out, then fold with a simple turn (letter fold). Roll out the dough again, then fold with a double turn (book fold). Roll it out again and finish by folding with a simple turn. Refrigerate for 30 minutes. Roll out the dough and cut out two 7-inch (18-cm) flowers with a pastry cutter. Refrigerate for 1 hour. Preheat the oven to 350°F (175°C/Gas Mark 4). Use a cookie cutter to cut out teardrop-shape holes from each of the petals and the center of one of the flaky brioche flowers. Place the two flowers on baking sheet lined with a Silpat mat. Cover with pie weights (baking beans) to keep the dough from puffing, then bake for 35 minutes.

FOR THE APPLE PRESSÉ

Peel and slice the apples with a mandoline. Place them in a square rimmed baking frame large enough to enable a 7-inch (18-cm)-diameter flower to be cut out. Bake in a static oven at 400°F (200°C/Gas Mark 6) for 1 hour.

FOR THE CARAMEL SAUCE

Make the caramel sauce as described on page 335.

FOR ASSEMBLY

Using a 7-inch (18-cm)-diameter flower-shape pastry ring to cut out the apple pressé. Cover it with a layer of caramel sauce. Lay it on the plain flaky brioche flower and cover with the perforated flower.

CRÊPE DENTELLE

3 large (UK medium/105 g) egg whites

¾ cup (90 g) confectioners' (icing) sugar

⅜ cup (45 g) all-purpose (plain) flour

3 tablespoons (45 g) unsalted butter

½ teaspoon (3 g) salt

According to preference: shredded coconut, pumpkin seeds, pine nuts, cocoa nibs, chopped pistachio nuts, chopped hazelnuts, etc.

Preheat the oven to 350°F (175°C/Gas Mark 4). In a large bowl, mix the egg whites with the sugar and flour. In the meantime, combine 2 cups (470 g) water with the butter and salt in a saucepan and bring to a boil. Pour this mixture into the bowl and incorporate. Spread the batter to a ¹/₁₆-inch (1-mm) thickness over a baking sheet covered with a Silpat mat. Add the flavoring of your choice. Bake for about 20 minutes. Once out of the oven, bring the four corners of the Silpat mat together toward the center to give shape to the flower. It will harden almost instantly. Caution: Wear heatproof gloves for this process!

MANDRiN

For the timut pepper ganache

See page 340

For the almond and mandarin dacquoise

2 extra-large (UK large/80 g) egg whites

3 tablespoons (35 g) superfine (caster) sugar

¾ cup (70 g) ground almonds

2 tablespoons (15 g) all-purpose (plain) flour

⅓ cup plus 2 tablespoons (55 g) confectioners' (icing) sugar

1 mandarin

For the yuzu gel

1½ tablespoons (20 g) superfine (caster) sugar

1⅛ teaspoons (3 g) agar powder

⅞ cup (200 g) yuzu juice

For the white chocolate coating

See page 338

For the mandarin and timut pepper insert

2 tablespoons (25 g) superfine (caster) sugar

3¾ teaspoons (10 g) agar powder

2 cups (500 g) fresh mandarin juice

3½ tablespoons (50 g) yuzu juice

1⅞ teaspoons (5 g) xanthan gum

1 tablespoon plus 2 teaspoons (10 g) timut peppercorns

¾ cup (165 g) candied mandarin

For finishing

3 mandarins

FOR THE TIMUT PEPPER GANACHE

Make the timut pepper ganache as described on page 340.

FOR THE YUZU GEL

Mix together the superfine sugar and agar powder. In a saucepan, bring the yuzu juice to a boil, then add the sugar and agar mixture. Incorporate using an immersion (stick) blender and refrigerate for about 1 hour, until set.

FOR THE MANDARIN AND TIMUT PEPPER INSERT

Mix together the superfine sugar and agar powder. In a saucepan, bring the mandarin juice to a boil, then add the sugar and agar mixture. Incorporate using an immersion blender and refrigerate for about 1 hour, until set. Blend the yuzu juice, xanthan gum, and timut peppercorns into the cold mixture. Incorporate the candied mandarin.

FOR THE ALMOND AND MANDARIN DACQUOISE

Preheat the oven to 340°F (170°C/Gas Mark 3½). Make a French meringue by beating the egg whites until stiff, incorporating the superfine sugar in three batches. The meringue is ready when it forms a peak on the end of the whisk without collapsing. Fold in the ground almonds, flour, and confectioners'sugar. Pipe the dacquoise batter into an 8-inch (20-cm)-diameter pastry ring. Peel the mandarin and separate into suprêmes. Arrange them on the batter and lightly press. Bake for 16 minutes.

FOR THE WHITE CHOCOLATE COATING

Make the white chocolate coating as described on page 338.

FOR ASSEMBLY

Whip the ganache with a hand mixer. Carefully lift off the pastry ring from the dacquoise. Transfer to a new pastry ring of the same diameter. Add a layer of the mandarin and timut pepper insert and a few dots of yuzu gel, making sure the new insert does not exceed a thickness of 1 inch (2.5 cm). Freeze for about 4 hours. Pipe ganache over the entire surface of a 7-inch (18-cm)-diameter Pavoni silicone entremets mold. Pipe more in the middle so the insert will be well centered. Add the insert and cover with ganache. Smooth with a spatula (palette knife). Freeze for about 6 hours, until set.

FOR PIPING

Use a pastry (piping) bag fitted with a size 125 tip (nozzle) to pipe wide ganache strips from the center to the edges, following the shape of the entremets. Freeze for about 3 hours.

FOR FINISHING

Peel the mandarins and separate the sections. Microwave for 15-30 seconds. Make a cut into the pith at the top of the sections and open the membrane outward to remove the flesh of each mandarin. Use a 3¼-inch (8-cm)-diameter cookie cutter to cut a disk from the center of the cake. Use a spray gun to uniformly flock the cake with the white chocolate coating. Add the mandarin pulp to the center of the entremets. Refrigerate for about 4 hours before serving.

For the sweet tart shell

See page 342

For the hazelnut crisp

¾ cup plus 1 tablespoon (250 g) hazelnut praline

1 cup (50 g) feuilletine flakes

2¾ teaspoons (12 g) cocoa butter

For the Paris-Brest cream

½ cup plus 1½ tablespoons (140 g) milk

¼ cup (60 g) whipping cream

1 teaspoon (2 g) vanilla pearls (or vanilla seeds)

2 large (UK medium/35 g) egg yolks

For the hazelnut dacquoise

2½ large (UK medium/80 g) egg whites (⅓ cup)

2 tablespoons (35 g) superfine (caster) sugar

⅞ cup (70 g) ground hazelnuts

2 tablespoons (15 g) all-purpose (plain) flour

⅓ cup plus 2 tablespoons (55 g) confectioners' (icing) sugar

1 mandarin

3 tablespoons (35 g) superfine (caster) sugar

1¾ teaspoons (10 g) custard powder

1½ tablespoons (10 g) all-purpose (plain) flour

4 tablespoons (60 g) unsalted butter

1 tablespoon (12 g) cocoa butter

5 teaspoons (28 g) gelatin mass (1¼ teaspoons/4 g gelatin powder hydrated in 5 teaspoons/24 g water)

2½ teaspoons (12 g) mascarpone cheese

½ cup (110 g) hazelnut paste

2 tablespoons (40 g) hazelnut praline

1 cup (120 g) whipped cream

For the hazelnut praline

See page 342

For the black lemon gel

¼ cup (50 g) superfine (caster) sugar

1 tablespoon (8 g) agar powder

2 cups (500 g) lemon juice

1⅞ teaspoons (5 g) xanthan gum

2½ teaspoons (12 g) black lemon powder

For assembly

Hazelnut praline

FOR THE SWEET TART SHELL

Make the tart shell (case) as described on page 342.

FOR THE HAZELNUT DACQUOISE

Make a French meringue by beating the egg whites until stiff, incorporating the superfine sugar in three batches. The meringue is ready when it forms a peak on the end of the whisk without collapsing. Fold in the ground hazelnuts, flour, and confectioners' sugar. Pipe the dacquoise batter into a 7-inch (18-cm)-diameter pastry ring. Peel the mandarin, removing all the pith, and separate the sections (segments). Arrange them on the batter and lightly press. Bake for 16 minutes.

FOR THE HAZELNUT PRALINE

Make the hazelnut praline as described on page 342.

FOR THE HAZELNUT CRISP

In a stand mixer fitted with a flat beater attachment, mix together hazelnut praline and feuilletine flakes while gradually adding the melted cocoa butter.

FOR THE PARIS-BREST CREAM

In a saucepan, combine the milk and cream with the vanilla pearls and bring to a boil. In the meantime, using a whisk, beat the yolks in a large bowl by whisking with the superfine sugar, custard powder, and flour until thick and pale. Pour the boiling mixture over the yolk mixture. Let boil for 2 minutes while stirring. Incorporate the butter, cocoa butter, gelatin mass, mascarpone, and the hazelnut paste and praline. Refrigerate for about 4 hours. In a stand mixer fitted with a whisk attachment, smooth the cream mixture, then add the whipped cream.

FOR THE BLACK LEMON GEL

Mix together the superfine sugar and agar powder. In a saucepan, bring the lemon juice to a boil. Add the sugar and agar mixture and incorporate using an immersion (stick) blender. Let cool. When the gel is cold, mix with an immersion blender, being careful not to beat in any air. Add the xanthan gum and black lemon powder. Mix everything together gently.

FOR ASSEMBLY

Spread a layer of crisp over the bottom of the tart shell. Make dots of hazelnut praliné and black lemon gel. Place the dacquoise disk on top.

FOR FINISHING

Whip the Paris-Brest cream with a hand mixer. Use a pastry (piping) bag fitted with a star tip (nozzle) to pipe interlocking strings over the tart in a continuous back-and-forth motion. The aim is to cover the entire surface to bring the cream "to life" while giving it a domelike volume.

TARTE
BOURDALOUE

For the flaky brioche

See page 335

For the almond cream

See page 336

For the pears in syrup

2½ cups (500 g) superfine (caster)
sugar
3 vanilla beans (pods), split and
scraped
15 small pears

For the kappa glaze

3½ teaspoons (45 g) glucose powder
3⅜ teaspoons (6 g) kappa
carrageenan
⅓ cup (65 g) superfine (caster)
sugar

ASSEMBLY

2 cups (200 g) slivered (flaked)
almonds
Confectioners' (icing) sugar

FOR THE FLAKY BRIOCHE

Make the flaky brioche as described on page 335.

FOR THE ALMOND CREAM

Make the almond cream as described on page 336.

FOR THE PEARS IN SYRUP

Make the syrup by combining 4¼ cups (1 kg) water with the superfine sugar and vanilla beans (pods) and seeds and bringing to a boil. Peel the whole pears. Give them a smooth and rounded appearance by rubbing them with a clean scouring pad and rinsing off any residue. Combine with the syrup and vanilla beans in a vacuum bag. Seal and cook sous-vide in an immersion circulator at 195°F (90°C) or in a pot of boiling water for 20 minutes. Drain then core 13 of the pears and keep 2 pears whole for assembly.

FOR THE KAPPA GLAZE

Mix together 1¾ cups (430 g) water and the glucose. In a saucepan, mix the kappa carrageenan with the superfine sugar. Add the water and glucose mixture. Bring to a boil for about 1 minute.

ASSEMBLY

Preheat the oven to 340°F (170°C/Gas Mark 3½). Fill the flaky brioche tart shell (case) halfway with almond cream. Sprinkle with the slivered almonds. Bake for about 8 minutes. Let cool for a few minutes. Dip the 13 cored pears into the hot kappa glaze and place them in an attractive arrangement on top. Halve one of the uncored pears and dust the other with confectioners'sugar. Arrange them in the center.

TiRAMiSU

For the coffee ganache

See page 338

For the ladyfingers

1¾ cups (220 g) all-purpose (plain) flour

⅓ cup (15 g) instant coffee powder

9 large eggs (450 g)

1⅛ cups (220 g) piloncillo (or superfine/caster) sugar

Superfine (caster) sugar

Confectioners' (icing) sugar

Espresso coffee

For the dark chocolate coating

See page 338

½ cup (100 g) cocoa butter

3½ ounces (100 g) semisweet (dark) chocolate

For the white chocolate coating

See page 338

For the mascarpone cream

1¼ cups (300 g) mascarpone cheese

1¼ cups (300 g) whipping cream

3 large eggs (225 g)

½ cup (90 g) piloncillo (or superfine/caster) sugar

1 tablespoon (15 g) Amaretto

FOR THE COFFEE GANACHE

Make the coffee ganache as described on page 338.

FOR THE LADYFINGER SPONGE DISKS

Preheat the oven to 400°F (200°C/Gas Mark 6). Sift the flour with the coffee powder. Separate the egg whites from the yolks. In a stand mixer fitted with a whisk attachment, beat the yolks with half the piloncillo sugar, then beat the whites with the other half. Mix everything together with the sifted flour and coffee. On a baking sheet lined with a Silpat mat, spread the batter to a ¾-inch (1-cm) thickness. Dust lightly with superfine sugar and confectioners' sugar. Bake for 5-6 minutes. Let cool, then cut out four disks with a diameter of 6¼ inches (16 cm), 4¾ inches (12 cm), 3¼ inches (8 cm), and 2½ inches (6 cm), respectively. Brush the disks with the espresso to soak.

FOR THE DARK AND WHITE CHOCOLATE COATINGS

Melt and pour the cocoa butter over the chopped dark chocolate. Incorporate using an immersion blender until smooth.

Make the white chocolate coating as described on p. 338.

FOR THE MASCARPONE CREAM

In a stand mixer fitted with a whisk attachment, whip all the ingredients to a mousselike consistency.

FOR ASSEMBLY

Whip the mascarpone cream with a hand mixer. Pipe mascarpone cream over the entire surface of a 7-inch (18-cm)-diameter Pavoni silicone entremets mold. Pipe more in the middle so the insert will be well centered. Insert the 3¼-inch (8-cm)-diameter sponge disk. Cover with a thin layer of mascarpone cream, then insert the 4¾-inch (12-cm) disk, cover again with mascarpone cream, and repeat the process with the 6¼-inch (16-cm) disk. Smooth with a spatula (palette knife). Freeze for about 6 hours, until set.

FOR FINISHING

Step 1
Gently unmold the entremets and place on a turntable. Use a pastry (piping) bag fitted with a size 125 Saint-Honoré tip (nozzle) to pipe small irregular waves of ganache over the top, starting from the center. Freeze for about 3 hours, until set. Use a 3¼-inch (8-cm)-diameter cookie cutter to make a hole in the center. Use a spray gun to cover the cake uniformly with the dark chocolate coating.

Step 2
Place the 2½-inch (6-cm)-diameter sponge disk on the turntable and repeat the same piping process as described in step 1. Use a spray gun to apply the white chocolate coating. Place this ganache-covered disk in the center of the entremets.

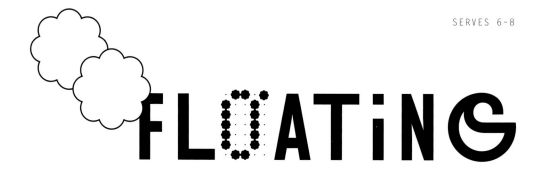

FLOATING iSLAND

For the crème anglaise

●

1 cup plus 3 tablespoons (285 g) milk

1 cup plus 3 tablespoons (285 g) whipping cream

1 vanilla bean (pod), split and scraped

5¼ large (UK medium/90 g) egg yolks

¼ cup (45 g) superfine (caster) sugar

¼ cup (45 g) piloncillo sugar

For the floating island

●

9 large (UK medium/300 g) egg whites

1 cup (200 g) superfine (caster) sugar

For assembly

●

Honey, melted

1 whole almond

FOR THE CRÈME ANGLAISE

In a saucepan, heat the milk combined with the cream and vanilla bean and seeds. In a large bowl, using a whisk, beat the egg yolks with the sugars until thick and pale. Add to the warm milk and cream mixture. Cook until the temperature reaches 193°F (84°C), then filter through a conical sieve and refrigerate.

FOR THE FLOATING iSLAND

Beat the egg whites, gradually adding the superfine sugar until stiff. Pour into a 7-inch (18-cm)-diameter flower-shape pastry ring. Microwave for 20 seconds, then for an additional 20 seconds, and finally for an additional 10 seconds. It is important to cook the meringue in three stages, opening the door and letting the steam out after every one. Carefully lift off the pastry ring.

FOR ASSEMBLY

Pour the crème anglaise into a dish. Place the flower in the center, drizzle with the melted honey, and position the almond in the center.

For the grape ganache

⅞ cup (200 g) whipping cream

5 large (UK medium/85 g) egg yolks

3½ tablespoons (40 g) superfine (caster) sugar

1 tablespoon (17 g) gelatin mass (¾ teaspoon/2.5 g gelatin powder hydrated in 1 tablespoon/14.5 g water)

⅔ cup (165 g) verjuice (sour grape juice)

⅔ cup (165 g) grape juice

1⅓ cups plus 1½ tablespoons (330 g) mascarpone cheese

For the sweet tart shell

See page 342

For the almond cream

See page 336

For the grape preserves

1⅓ cups (200 g) green grapes

1⅓ cups (200 g) black grapes

2½ tablespoons (40 g) grape puree

1 drizzle olive oil

2½ tablespoons (30 g) superfine (caster) sugar

2 tablespoons (30 g) glucose powder

1½ teaspoons (6 g) pectin NH

⅜ teaspoon (2 g) tartaric acid

For the grape gel

2½ cups (500 g) grape puree

¼ cup (50 g) superfine (caster) sugar

3¾ teaspoons (10 g) agar powder

2¼ teaspoons (6 g) xanthan gum

1⅔ cups (250 g) green grapes

1⅔ cups (250 g) black grapes

For the purple chocolate coating

½ cup (100 g) cocoa butter

3½ ounces (100 g) white chocolate, chopped

1 teaspoon (5 g) red fat-soluble food coloring

scant ¼ teaspoon (1 g) blue fat-soluble food coloring

scant ⅛ teaspoon (0.5 g) red water-soluble food coloring

For the green chocolate coating

See page 338

For the kappa glaze

⅓ cup (65 g) superfine (caster) sugar

3⅜ teaspoons (6 g) kappa carrageenan

3½ tablespoons (45 g) glucose powder

For the mock grapes

Confectioners' (icing) sugar

FOR THE GRAPE GANACHE

Bring the cream to a boil. Beat the yolks with the superfine sugar. Pour a little boiling cream over this mixture, then return it to the saucepan to make a crème anglaise. Cook for 2 minutes, then incorporate the gelatin mass, verjuice, and grape juice using an immersion (stick) blender. Filter through a conical sieve and add the mascarpone. Refrigerate for about 12 hours.

FOR THE SWEET TART SHELL

Make the tart shell (case) as described on page 342.

FOR THE ALMOND CREAM

Make the almond cream as described on page 336.

FOR THE GRAPE PRESERVES

In a saucepan, caramelize the grapes and grape puree with the olive oil. Simmer over low heat for about 30 minutes. Add the superfine sugar, glucose, pectin, and tartaric acid. Mix well and bring to a boil for 1 minute. Refrigerate until set.

FOR THE GRAPE GEL

Mix together the superfine sugar and agar powder. Heat the grape puree in a saucepan. Add the sugar and agar mixture. Let cool. Incorporate the xanthan gum using an immersion blender, then quarter the grapes and stir them into the gel.

FOR THE PURPLE CHOCOLATE COATING

In a saucepan, melt the cocoa butter, then pour it over the chopped chocolate. Using an immersion blender, incorporate the food colorings, blending until smooth.

FOR THE GREEN CHOCOLATE COATING

Make the green chocolate coating as described on page 338.

FOR THE KAPPA GLAZE

Mix together the sugar and kappa carrageenan. In a saucepan, combine 1¾ cups (430 g) water with the glucose, and the superfine sugar and carrageenan mixture, and bring to a boil.

FOR THE MOCK GRAPES

Whip the ganache with a hand mixer. Pour the grape gel into ¾-inch (2-cm)-diameter spherical silicone molds. Freeze for about 3 hours until set. Carefully unmold. Fill the bottom of 1¼-inch (3-cm)-diameter spherical silicone molds with the whipped ganache. Add the insert, then cover with ganache. Freeze for about 3 hours until set. Smooth the surface of the grapes before dipping half in the purple chocolate coating and the other half in the green chocolate coating. Let harden. Dip the mock grapes in the kappa glaze and lightly dust with confectioners' sugar. Let the glaze harden and proceed to assemble the tart.

FOR ASSEMBLY

Preheat the oven to 340°F (170°C/Gas Mark 3½). Spread a thin layer of almond and vanilla cream inside the tart shell. Cut four green grapes and four black grapes in half and add them on top of the cream. Bake for 8 minutes and let cool for about 15 minutes. Add a layer of grape preserves, then fill the tart shell completely with grape gel and smooth the surface. Make an attractive arrangement with the mock and real grapes over the top.

PANUT

For the sweet tart shell

See page 342

For the peanut praline

3½ cups (500 g) peanuts

⅔ cup (125 g) superfine (caster) sugar

2½ teaspoons (10 g) fleur de sel

For the peanut crisp

1¾ cups (250 g) peanuts

1⅔ cups (500 g) peanut praline

2 cups (100 g) feuilletine flakes

2 tablespoons (25 g) cocoa butter

For the peanut sponge cake

½ cup (1 stick/120 g) unsalted butter

½ cup (140 g) peanut butter

8½ extra-large (UK large/160 g) egg yolks (⅔ cup)

1 cup (180 g) superfine (caster) sugar

6½ extra-large (UK large/240 g) egg whites (1 cup)

2 tablespoons (15 g) all-purpose (plain) flour

1½ tablespoons (15 g) potato starch

Chopped peanuts

For the caramel sauce

See page 335

For the caramelized peanuts

2¾ cups (400 g) peanuts

⅔ cup (120 g) superfine (caster) sugar

⅜ teaspoon (2 g) tartaric acid

FOR THE SWEET TART SHELL

Make the tart shell (case) as described on page 342.

FOR THE PEANUT PRALINE

Roast the peanuts in the oven at 325°F (165°C/Gas Mark 3) for 15 minutes.
Make a dry caramel with the sugar. Let cool, then process to a paste.
Grind the peanuts. In a stand mixer fitted with a flat beater, combine the
peanuts, caramel, sugar, and salt and mix thoroughly.

FOR THE PEANUT CRISP

Roast the peanuts in the oven at 325°F (165°C/Gas Mark 3) for 15 minutes,
then chop them. In a stand mixer fitted with a flat beater attachment,
mix together the peanuts, praline, and feuilletine flakes while gradually
adding the melted cocoa butter.

FOR THE PEANUT SPONGE

Preheat the oven to 175°F (80°C). In a stand mixer fitted with a flat
beater attachment, beat the butter with the peanut butter. Using a whisk,
beat together the yolks with 1/3 cup (60 g) of the sugar until thick and
pale. Beat the egg whites until stiff with the remaining sugar. Combine
the three mixtures. Sift together the flour and starch and incorporate.
On a baking sheet lined with a Silpat mat, spread a thin layer of the
batter and sprinkle with the chopped peanuts. Bake for 13 minutes.

FOR THE CARAMEL SAUCE

Make the caramel sauce as described on page 335.

FOR THE CARAMELIZED PEANUTS

Roast the peanuts in the oven at 340°F (170°C/Gas Mark 3½) for 15 minutes.
In a saucepan, heat the sugar, 1/3 cup (50 g) water, and the tartaric acid
until it turns into a dark caramel. Add the peanuts. Let caramelize for a
few minutes, then transfer to a baking sheet lined with a Silpat mat. Space
the peanuts apart to prevent them from sticking together.

FOR ASSEMBLY

Spread a layer of the crisp inside the tart shell. Cover with a peanut
sponge disk, cut to fit, then fill to the top with caramel sauce and
smooth with a spatula (palette knife). Arrange the caramelized peanuts in
a rosette pattern.

MiLLEFEUiLLE

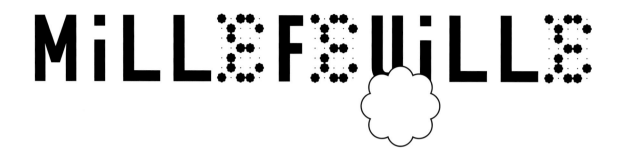

For the vanilla ganache

3 cups (700 g) whipping cream

1 vanilla bean (pod)

5¼ ounces (150 g) white couverture chocolate

2 tablespoons (36 g) gelatin mass (1½ teaspoons/5 g gelatin powder hydrated in 2 tablespoons/31 g water)

For the flaky brioche

⅞ cup (200 g) milk

1¼ small cakes (25 g) fresh yeast, or 4⅜ teaspoons active dry (easy-blend) yeast, dissolved in milk or water

4 cups (550 g) bread (strong) flour

1⅜ teaspoons (8 g) salt

3½ tablespoons (40 g superfine (caster) sugar

2 large (UK medium/100 g) eggs

3½ tablespoons (50 g) unsalted butter, softened

2¼ cups (500 g) unsalted dry butter (84% fat content)

For the caramel sauce

Double the ingredients on page 335.

For the chocolate fondant

1 pound (500 g) fondant

⅓ cup (60 g) cocoa butter

3 tablespoons plus 2 teaspoons (50 g) glucose powder

1¾ ounces (50 g) milk chocolate

1¾ ounces (50 g) white chocolate

1¾ ounces (50 g) semisweet (dark) chocolate

1 pinch charcoal black food coloring

FOR THE VANILLA GANACHE

Make the vanilla ganache as described on page 340.

FOR THE FLAKY BRIOCHE

In a stand mixer fitted with a dough hook, combine the milk, yeast, flour, salt, and sugar and mix on speed 1 while gradually adding the eggs. Increase to speed 2 and continue mixing until the dough pulls away from the sides. Cut the softened butter into cubes, add to the dough, and knead until the dough is smooth. Let the dough rise at room temperature (68-77°F/20-25°C) for about 1 hour. Use your palms to flatten and deflate the dough, then roll out into a rectangle. Shape the dry butter into a rectangle half the size and place it in the center of the dough. Fold over the sides of the dough to encase the butter and roll out, then fold with a simple turn (letter fold). Roll out the dough again, then fold with a double turn (book fold). Roll it out again and finish by folding with a simple turn. Refrigerate for 10 minutes. Roll out the dough and use it to line four 7-inch (18-cm)-diameter flower-shape baking pans lined with parchment (baking) paper (or use the one pan and bake four times). Refrigerate for 1 hour. Cover the dough with more parchment paper. Fill with pie weights (baking beans) to ensure the brioche retains the shape of the pan. Bake at 350°F (175°C/Gas Mark 4) for 15 minutes.

FOR THE CARAMEL SAUCE

In a saucepan, heat the sugar and ½ cup (110 g) of the glucose to 365°F (185°C) and cook to an amber caramel. In another saucepan, heat the milk and cream with the remaining glucose, vanilla, and fleur de sel. Deglaze the caramel with the hot milk mixture. Cook until the temperature reaches 220°F (105°C), then filter through a conical sieve. Add the butter when the caramel cools to 158°F (70°C) and incorporate using an immersion (stick) blender.

FOR THE CHOCOLATE FONDANT

In a saucepan, heat the fondant to 96.8°F (36°C), then add the cocoa butter and glucose. Melt the three chocolates separately. Add the charcoal black coloring to the semisweet (dark) chocolate.

FOR ASSEMBLY

Whip the ganache with a hand mixer. Use a pastry (piping) bag fitted with a size 20 plain tip (nozzle) to pipe a ball of ganache in each petal of a flaky brioche flower as well as one in the center. Fill all the spaces with caramel sauce. Repeat this process two times. Transfer the millefeuille to a rack and cover the last flaky brioche flower with fondant. Remove the excess with a spatula (palette knife). To decorate, use a pastry bag fitted with a size 1 plain tip to pipe rosettes patterns in melted semisweet, milk, and white chocolates.

GÂTEAU

BASQUE

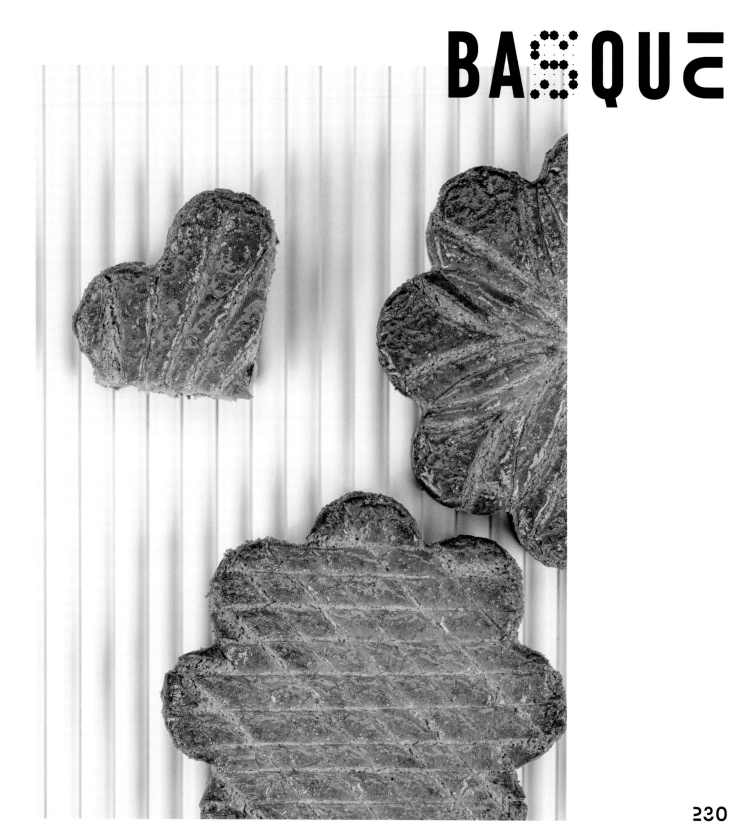

For the vanilla pastry cream

●

See page 336

For the cherry insert

●

4 tablespoons (60 g) unsalted
butter

$\frac{1}{3}$ cup (60 g) superfine (caster)
sugar

$\frac{2}{3}$ cup (60 g) ground almonds

1 tablespoon (10 g) potato starch

1 jumbo (UK large/60 g) egg

$\frac{1}{2}$ cup (120 g) vanilla pastry cream

2 tablespoons (25 g) nut paste
(almonds and hazelnuts)

15 fresh cherries, pitted and
halved

For the Basque shortbread

●

$\frac{3}{4}$ cup plus 1 tablespoon (1$\frac{5}{8}$ sticks/
180 g) unsalted butter

$\frac{3}{4}$ cup (160 g) packed brown sugar

1$\frac{1}{4}$ large (UK medium/65 g) eggs
($\frac{1}{4}$ cup)

$\frac{3}{8}$ teaspoon (2 g) salt

2$\frac{5}{8}$ teaspoons (12 g) baking powder

1$\frac{3}{4}$ cups (220 g) all-purpose (plain)
flour

1$\frac{1}{8}$ cups (110 g) ground almonds

For the egg wash

●

3$\frac{1}{2}$ large (UK medium/60 g) egg yolks
($\frac{1}{4}$ cup)

4 teaspoons (20 g) whipping cream

3$\frac{1}{2}$ teaspoons (25 g) honey

FOR THE VANILLA PASTRY CREAM

Make the vanilla pastry cream as described on page 336.

FOR THE CHERRY INSERT

In a stand mixer fitted with flat beater attachment, cream the butter with the superfine sugar, ground almonds, and starch. Gradually incorporate the egg, followed by the pastry cream and nut paste. Use your fingers to lightly press the cherries into the mixture. Put the mixture into a 5½-inch (14-cm)-diameter and 1-inch (2.5-cm)-deep pastry ring. Freeze for 4 hours.

FOR THE BASQUE SHORTBREAD

In a stand mixer fitted with a flat beater attachment, mix the butter with the brown sugar until crumbly. Incorporate the eggs, followed by the salt, baking powder, flour, and ground almonds, and mix until smooth. Roll out the dough to an ⅛-inch (3-mm) thickness. Line a 7-inch (18-cm)-diameter flower-shape baking pan previously lined with parchment (baking) paper.

FOR THE EGG WASH

Mix all the ingredients together.

FOR ASSEMBLY

Preheat the oven to 340°F (170°C/Gas Mark 3½). Place the insert inside the Basque shortbread pie shell (case). Cover with a sheet of dough cut into a star shape and trim to the shape of the baking pan. Decorate the top of the pie by scoring the dough with a knife tip and brushing lightly with egg wash. Bake for 35 minutes.

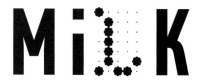

For the sweet tart shell

See page 342

For the caramel sauce

See page 335

For the vanilla praline

●

1 cup (150 g) almonds

1 vanilla bean (pod)

½ cup (100 g) superfine (caster) sugar

5 ⅓ cups (75 g) puffed rice

For the rice pudding

3 ⅓ cups (800 g) milk

⅓ cup (70 g) superfine (caster) sugar

½ cup (100 g) Carnaroli rice

2 teaspoons (4 g) vanilla pearls (or vanilla seeds)

¾ cup (2 g) xanthan gum

For the milk foam

5 teaspoons (28 g) gelatin mass (¾ teaspoon/4 g gelatin powder hydrated in 5 teaspoons/24 g water)

4 ⅛ cups (1 kg) milk

2 teaspoons (5 g) Sucro emulsifier

FOR THE SWEET TART SHELL

Make the tart shell (case) as described on page 342.

FOR THE CARAMEL SAUCE

Make the caramel sauce as described on page 335.

FOR THE VANILLA PRALINE

Roast the almonds and vanilla bean (pod) in the oven at 325°F (165°C/ Gas Mark 3) for 15 minutes. In a saucepan, heat the sugar and ¼ cup plus 2 teaspoons (70 g) water to 230°F (110°C). Add the almonds and vanilla bean, stir to coat well in the syrup, and let caramelize. Cool the caramel completely before processing to a paste in a food processor. Mix in the puffed rice.

FOR THE RICE PUDDING

In a saucepan, combine the milk with the sugar, rice, and vanilla pearls and bring to a boil. Keep at a boil for about 12 minutes. The rice grains should be cooked through but still firm. Drain the rice, collecting the milk. Add the xanthan gum to the milk. Mix the rice with the milk.

FOR THE MILK FOAM

Melt the gelatin mass in a microwave. In a mixing beaker or bowl, use an immersion (stick) blender to whip the milk with the emulsifier and gelatin mass to a foam.

FOR ASSEMBLY

Pipe a thin layer of vanilla praline in the tart shell (case). Fill the shell to three-quarters with rice pudding. Fill to the top with caramel sauce, then spoon the milk foam over the tart.

WINTER

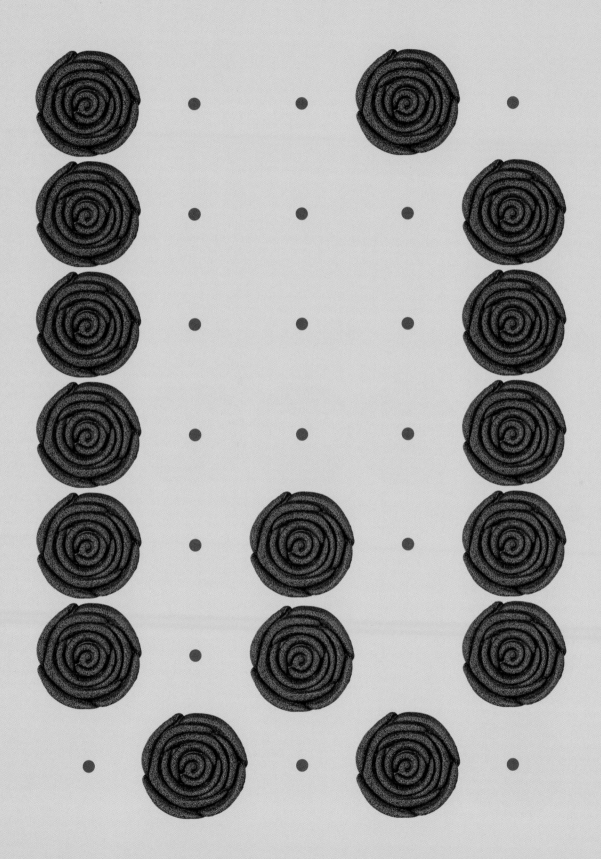

FLOWER XXL

For the cinnamon ganache

6½ cups (1.56 kg) whipping cream

4 cinnamon sticks

3 tablespoons (20 g) ground cinnamon

12½ ounces (350 g) ivory white couverture chocolate, chopped

¼ cup plus 1 tablespoon (80 g) gelatin mass (4⅝ teaspoons/14 g gelatin powder hydrated in ¼ cup plus 1 tablespoons/66 g water)

For the speculoos tart shell

1 cup (2 sticks/225 g) unsalted butter

1⅛ cups (145 g) confectioners' (icing) sugar

½ cup (45 g) ground hazelnuts

⅜ teaspoon (2 g) salt

1¾ large (UK medium/87 g) eggs (⅓ cup)

2¾ cups (375 g) bread (strong) flour

¾ cup (120 g) potato starch

¼ cup (30 g) ground cinnamon

For the almond and cinnamon cream

1⅛ cups (2¼ sticks/250 g) unsalted butter, softened

1¼ cups (250 g) superfine (caster) sugar

⅞ cup (100 g) ground cinnamon

2⅔ cups (250 g) ground almonds

5 large (UK medium/250 g) eggs

For the grapefruit gel

4 cups (1 kg) grapefruit juice

½ cup (100 g) superfine (caster) sugar

5⅜ teaspoons (15 g) agar powder

1⅞ teaspoons (5 g) xanthan gum

½ cup plus 1 tablespoon (100 g) candied grapefruit peel

scant ½ cup (100 g) grapefruit suprêmes, finely diced

For the ruby chocolate coating

See page 338

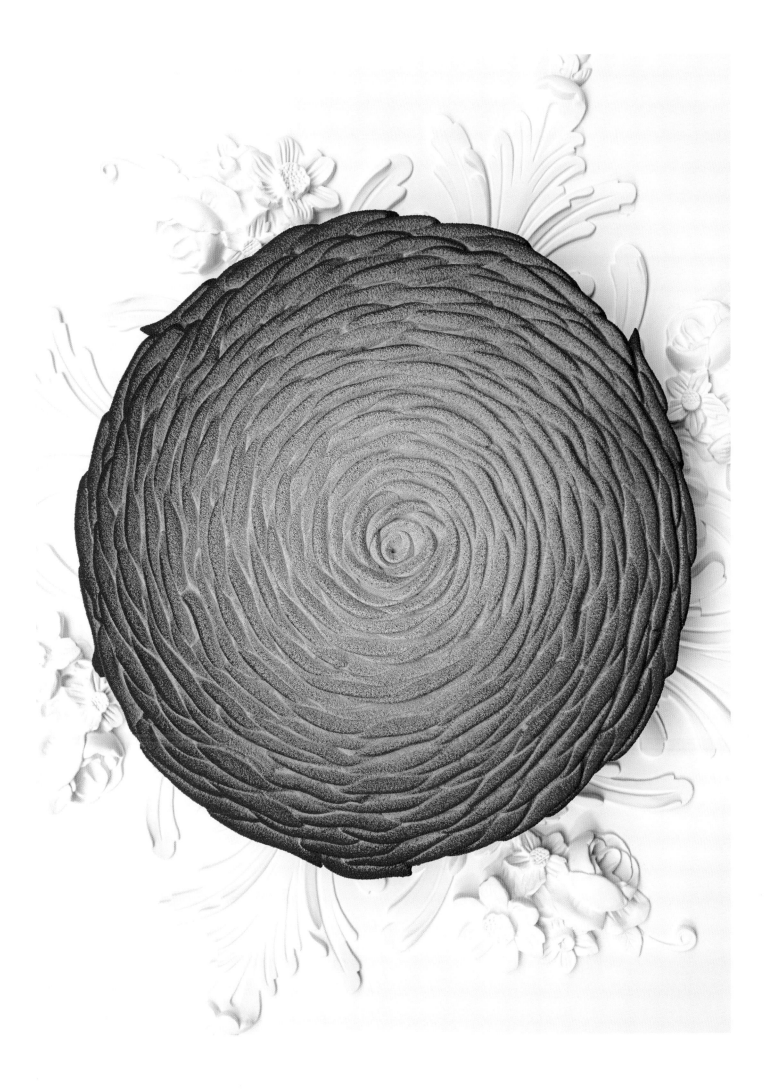

FOR THE CINNAMON GANACHE

The previous day, heat half the cream in a saucepan. Add the cinnamon sticks and ground cinnamon. Remove from the heat, cover, and let infuse for about 10 minutes. Heat the mixture again and filter through a conical sieve. Pour it over the chopped chocolate and gelatin mass, then add the remaining cream. Incorporate using an immersion (stick) blender until the ganache is smooth. Refrigerate for about 12 hours.

FOR THE SPECULOOS TART SHELL

Preheat the oven to 325°F (165°C/Gas Mark 3). In a stand mixer fitted with a flat beater, cream the butter with the confectioners' sugar, ground hazelnuts, and salt. Add and beat in the eggs, then add the flour, starch, and cinnamon. Mix until smooth. Refrigerate until chilled. Roll out the dough to an ⅛-inch (3-mm) thickness and cut out a 24-inch (60-cm)-diameter disk. Line a 15½-inch (40-cm)-diameter pastry ring. Trim off the excess with a knife. Place the ring on a Silpat mat (or parchment/baking paper). Prick the tart shell (case) with a fork. Bake for 30 minutes.

FOR THE ALMOND AND CINNAMON CREAM

In a stand mixer fitted with a flat beater attachment, cream the butter with the superfine sugar, cinnamon, and ground almonds. Gradually incorporate the eggs, then refrigerate.

FOR THE GRAPEFRUIT GEL

In a saucepan, bring the grapefruit juice to a boil. Mix together the superfine sugar, agar powder, and xanthan gum, then add to the juice. Incorporate using an immersion blender, then refrigerate until set. When set, blend the gel again and add the candied grapefruit and the finely diced suprêmes.

FOR THE RUBY CHOCOLATE COATING

Make the ruby chocolate coating as described on page 338.

FOR ASSEMBLY

Preheat the oven to 340°F (170°C/Gas Mark 3½). Fill the tart shell with the almond and cinnamon cream. Bake for 8 minutes. Let cool for about 15 minutes, then fill to the top with grapefruit gel. Refrigerate for about 30 minutes.

FOR FINISHING

Whip the ganache with a hand mixer. Using a metal stand and a pastry (piping) bag fitted with a size 125 Saint-Honoré tip (nozzle), and starting from the center, pipe irregular petals with the whipped ganache to create a pretty flower. Pipe short semicircular lines from left to right. Use a spray gun to flock the tart with the ruby chocolate coating, creating an ombré effect by going from deep pink to light pink.

COFFEE

For the coffee ganache

2⅓ cups (550 g) whipping cream

⅙ cup (28 g) coffee beans

3½ ounces (100 g) ivory white couverture chocolate, chopped

1½ tablespoons (24 g) gelatin mass (1¼ teaspoons/4 g gelatin powder hydrated in 1½ tablespoons/24 g water)

2 tablespoons (6 g) instant coffee powder

For the hazelnut crisp

¾ cup (100 g) hazelnuts

1⅙ cups (100 g) Alain Ducasse coffee beans

3 tablespoons (35 g) superfine (caster) sugar

2 cups (100 g) feuilletine flakes

2 teaspoons (10 g) grapeseed oil

2¼ teaspoons (10 g) cocoa butter

For the sweet tart shell

See page 342

For the milk coffee preserves

¾ cup (240 g) sweetened condensed milk

1 cup (240 g) evaporated milk

1½ teaspoon (4 g) xanthan gum

¼ cup (14 g) instant coffee powder

For the coffee dacquoise

2 extra-large (UK large/75 g) egg whites

3 tablespoons (35 g) superfine (caster) sugar

¾ cup (70 g) ground almonds

2 tablespoons (15 g) all-purpose (plain) flour

⅓ cup plus 2 tablespoons (55 g) confectioners' (icing) sugar

2 tablespoons (6 g) instant coffee powder

For the coffee glaze

⅓ cup (100 g) neutral glaze
2 teaspoons (2 g) instant coffee powder

FOR THE COFFEE GANACHE

The previous day, heat half the cream in a saucepan. Add the coffee beans. Process using an immersion blender, then remove from the heat, cover, and let infuse for about 10 minutes. Heat the mixture again and filter through a conical sieve. Pour it over the chopped chocolate and gelatin mass, then add the remaining cream. Incorporate the coffee powder using an immersion blender until the ganache is smooth. Refrigerate for about 12 hours.

FOR THE HAZELNUT CRISP

Preheat the oven to 325°F (165°C/Gas Mark 3). Roast the hazelnuts and coffee beans in the oven for 15 minutes. Make a dry caramel with the superfine sugar; it should make 1½ tablespoons (30 g). Let cool until solid. Use an immersion (stick) blender to process, separately, the feuilletine flakes, followed by the caramel, then finally the hazelnuts with the coffee beans while gradually incorporating the oil. In a stand mixer fitted with a flat beater attachment, mix all the ingredients together while gradually adding the melted cocoa butter.

FOR THE SWEET TART SHELL

Make the tart shell (case) as described on page 342.

FOR THE MILK COFFEE PRESERVES

In a copper saucepan, caramelize the condensed milk in the oven at 195°F (90°C) for 4 hours. Combine the caramelized milk, evaporated milk, xanthan gum, and coffee powder and blend together with an immersion (stick) blender.

FOR THE COFFEE DACQUOISE

Preheat the oven to 340°F (170°C/Gas Mark 3½). Make a French meringue by beating the egg whites until stiff, incorporating the superfine sugar in three batches. The meringue is ready when it forms a peak on the end of the whisk without collapsing. Fold in the ground almonds, flour, confectioners' sugar, and coffee powder. Pipe the dacquoise batter into an 8-inch (20-cm)-diameter pastry ring. Bake for 16 minutes.

FOR THE MILK COFFEE PRESERVES INSERT

Pipe the milk coffee preserves into a 1¼-inch (3-cm)-diameter hemispherical mold and freeze for 3 hours, until set.

FOR ASSEMBLY

Fill the tart shell halfway with the hazelnut crisp. Fill to four-fifths with the milk coffee preserves. Lift off the pastry ring from the dacquoise and trim its diameter by ⅜-¾ inch (1-2 cm) to make piping easier. Insert the dacquoise disk, leaving it flush with the top edge of the tart shell. Insert a toothpick (cocktail stick) into the frozen insert and dip in the milk chocolate coating. Place in the center of the tart.

FOR FINISHING

Whip the ganache with a hand mixer. Using a metal stand and a pastry (piping) bag fitted with a size 104 Saint-Honoré tip (nozzle), and starting from the center, pipe uniform petals with the whipped ganache to create a pretty flower. Pipe in a circular motion from left to right around the insert to make ¾-inch (2-cm) semicircular petals in the middle, then gradually increase the size of the semicircles and start each petal in the middle of the preceding one.

FOR THE COFFEE GLAZE

In a saucepan, combine the neutral glaze with the coffee powder and bring to a boil. Transfer the mixture to a spray gun and flock the tart with glaze. Finish with a light coating of glaze on the insert.

TATiN

For the flaky brioche
❁
See page 335

For the almond cream
❁
See page 336

For the caramel sauce
❁
Double the ingredients on page 335.

For the Japanese crabapples
❁
15 (500 g) Japanese crabapples
1¼ cups (250 g) superfine (caster) sugar

FOR THE FLAKY BRiOCHE

Make the flaky brioche tart shell (case) as described on page 335.

FOR THE ALMOND CREAM

Make the almond cream as described on page 336.

FOR THE CARAMEL SAUCE

Make the caramel sauce as described on page 335.

FOR THE JAPANESE CRABAPPLES

Preheat the oven to 350°F (175°C/Gas Mark 4). Wash the crabapples and place on a baking sheet lined with a Silpat mat. Bake for 5 minutes. Make a dry caramel with the sugar. After taking them out of the oven, let the crabapples cool slightly before dipping them into the caramel to glaze.

FOR ASSEMBLY

Preheat the oven to 325°F (165°C/Gas Mark 3). Fill the tart shell with almond cream. Bake for 8 minutes. Let cool for about 15 minutes. Add a generous layer of caramel sauce, then make an attractive arrangement with the caramelized crabapples.

MANGO

For the sweet tart shell

●

See page 342

For the mango gel

●

1 cup (200 g) mango puree
1 cup (200 g) passion fruit juice
2 teaspoons (5 g) xanthan gum

For the vanilla pastry cream

●

See page 336

For the almond and vanilla cream

●

See page 336

For the vanilla glaze

●

See page 341

For assembly

●

2 mangoes

FOR THE SWEET TART SHELL

Make the tart shell (case) as described on page 342.

FOR THE VANILLA PASTRY CREAM

Make the vanilla pastry cream as described on page 336.

FOR THE ALMOND AND VANILLA CREAM

Make the almond and vanilla cream as described on page 336.

FOR THE MANGO GEL

Combine all the ingredients and incorporate using an immersion (stick) blender until the mixture thickens.

FOR THE VANILLA GLAZE

Make the vanilla glaze as described on page 341.

FOR ASSEMBLY

Preheat the oven to 340°F (170°C/Gas Mark 3½). Peel and halve the mangoes, running the knife as closely as possible to the pit (stone). Thinly slice the flesh with a knife and cut the scraps (trimmings) into cubes. Fill the tart shell with almond and vanilla cream and bake for 8 minutes. Let cool for about 15 minutes. Pipe a ball of pastry cream at the center of the tart to serve as a reference point. Pipe a ball of pastry cream at the edge of the tart and continue inward to make a strip reaching the ball at the center. Repeat the process with the mango gel. Continue until the tart is completely filled. The aim is to cover the tart with alternating white and orange bands. Distribute the mango cubes evenly over the filling and smooth with a spatula (palette knife), then arrange the mango slices over the top in a rosette pattern. To create volume, lightly press the mango slices in the outer ring into the tart. Gradually tilt the angle of the following slices so that they are almost upright by the third or fourth ring. Use a spray gun to lightly flock the tart with vanilla glaze.

GiANDUJA

For the gianduja ganache

1 ⅓ cups plus 1½ tablespoons (340 g) whipping cream

7 tablespoons (100 g) unsalted butter

⅓ cup plus 2 tablespoons (100 g) gianduja

9½ ounces (270 g) Alain Ducasse dark chocolate, chopped

For the chocolate choux puffs

⅓ cup (30 g) unsweetened cocoa powder

½ extra-large (UK large/20 g) egg white (4 teaspoons)

3½ tablespoons (50 g) milk

⅜ teaspoon (2 g) salt

1 teaspoon (4 g) superfine (caster) sugar

For the chocolate tart shell

See page 342

3 tablespoons (45 g) unsalted butter

⅓ cup plus 1 tablespoon (55 g) bread (strong) flour

2 medium (UK small/90 g) eggs

For the hazelnut praline

See page 342

For assembly

1⅞ cups (400 g) gianduja

2¼ teaspoons (10 g) cocoa butter

FOR THE GIANDUJA GANACHE

The previous day, bring half the cream to a boil in a saucepan. Combine the butter with the gianduja and chopped chocolate and pour the hot cream over the mixture. Add the remaining cream and incorporate using an immersion (stick) blender until the ganache is smooth. Filter through a conical sieve and refrigerate for about 12 hours.

FOR THE CHOCOLATE TART SHELL

Make the chocolate tart shell (case) as described on page 342.

FOR THE HAZELNUT PRALINE

Make the hazelnut praline as described on page 342.

FOR THE CHOCOLATE CHOUX PUFFS

Mix the cocoa powder with the egg whites. In a saucepan, combine 3½ tablespoons (50 g) water with the milk, salt, sugar, and butter and bring to a boil. Let boil for 1-2 minutes, then add the flour and stir over low heat until the paste pulls away easily from the sides of the pan. Transfer to a stand mixer fitted with a flat beater attachment. Mix to release the steam, then add the eggs in three batches. Incorporate the cocoa mixture. Refrigerate for about 2 hours. On a baking sheet lined with a Silpat mat (or parchment/baking paper), pipe ¾-inch (2-cm)-diameter choux puffs. Bake in a deck oven at 350°F (175°C) for 30 minutes (or for a conventional oven, preheat the oven to 500°F/260°C/Gas Mark 10, introduce the baking sheet and turn off the oven for 15 minutes, then turn it back on and continue baking at 325°F/160°C/Gas Mark 3 for 10 minutes).

FOR ASSEMBLY

Fill the choux puffs with 1⅜ cups (300 g) gianduja. Mix the remaining ½ cup (100 g) with the melted cocoa butter. Spread a layer of praline in the tart shell, filling to two-thirds. Distribute ten gianduja-filled choux puffs over the praline. Fill in the empty spaces with the gianduja and cocoa butter mixture. Refrigerate for 1 hour.

FOR FINISHING

Use a pastry (piping) bag fitted with a size 104 tip (nozzle) to pipe the ganache in a continuous back-and-forth motion over the tart. The aim is to cover the entire surface with interlinked ribbon loops that bring the ganache "to life."

LYCHEE

For the lychee and verbena pepper ganache

✿

See page 340

For the lychee centers

✿

2⅓ cups (600 g) lychee puree

⅓ cup (60 g) superfine (caster) sugar

2¼ teaspoons (6 g) agar powder

1⅛ teaspoons (3 g) xanthan gum

¾ cup (170 g) aloe vera

⅓ cup (10 g) food-safe marigold flowers

1¾ pounds (830 g) lychees

For the pink chocolate coating

✿

See page 338

For the green chocolate coating

✿

See page 338

For the white chocolate coating

✿

See page 338

For the lychee coating

✿

Non-melting snow white topping sugar, such as Codineige or King Arthur

FOR THE LYCHEE AND VERBENA PEPPER GANACHE

Make the lychee and verbena pepper ganache as described on page 340.

FOR THE LYCHEE CENTERS

In a saucepan, bring the lychee puree to a boil, then mix together the sugar and agar powder and add to the puree. Refrigerate until set, then use an immersion (stick) blender to loosen the gel. Add the xanthan gum; aloe vera, cut into cubes; the marigolds, finely chopped; and the lychees, quartered. Pour into 3¼-inch (8-cm)-long oval (calisson-shape) silicone molds. Place in the freezer to make the centers. Carefully unmold.

FOR PIPING

Whip the ganache with a hand mixer. Cut off the end off a tipless pastry (piping) bag and improvise a Saint-Honoré tip (nozzle) by cutting a $^1/_{16}$-inch (2-mm) notch. Pipe small, uniform flames of ganache over each frozen center, starting at one end and working toward the other, following their shape.

FOR THE PINK, GREEN, AND WHITE CHOCOLATE COATINGS

Make the three different coatings as described on page 338.

FOR THE LYCHEE COATING

Drizzle a horizontal line of green coating across the middle of the pink chocolate coating, then form random patches of white coating. Insert toothpicks (cocktail sticks) into the frozen centers and dip them into the coating mixture at 86°F (30°C), leaving a green line in the middle of the mock lychees. Gently lift the sculpted fruit from the coating for an ombré effect. Let harden for 1-2 minutes, then lightly dust with snow sugar. Refrigerate for about 4 hours before serving.

CHOCOLATE

For the chocolate ganache

●

2 ⅓ cups (550 g) whipping cream

1¾ ounces (50 g) bittersweet (dark) chocolate (66% cocoa), chopped

3¾ teaspoons (21 g) gelatin mass (1 teaspoon/3 g gelatin powder hydrated in 3¾ teaspoons/18 g water)

For the chocolate tart shell

●

See page 342

For the cocoa nib praline

●

⅔ cup (100 g) hazelnuts

2½ tablespoons (30 g) superfine (caster) sugar

⅓ cup (40 g) cocoa nibs

3 tablespoons (40 g) grapeseed oil

½ teaspoon (2 g) fleur de sel

For the chocolate-caramel sauce

●

¼ cup (50 g) superfine (caster) sugar

⅜ cup (80 g) glucose powder

½ cup (130 g) milk

½ cup plus 1 tablespoon (135 g) whipping cream

½ teaspoon (2 g) fleur de sel

2¾ tablespoons (40 g) unsalted butter

1¾ ounces (50 g) Alain Ducasse dark chocolate, chopped

For the chocolate sponge cake

●

1 cup (100 g) ground almonds

⅓ cup plus 1 tablespoon (90 g) packed brown sugar

⅓ cup (40 g) all-purpose (plain) flour

⅞ teaspoon (4 g) baking powder

1⅛ teaspoons (10 g) unsweetened cocoa powder

⅞ teaspoon (5 g) salt

4 large (UK medium/135 g) egg whites

2 ⅓ large (UK medium/40 g egg yolks (2 tablespoons plus 2 teaspoons)

1½ tablespoons (25 g) whipping cream

2¾ tablespoons (40 g) unsalted butter, melted

1½ tablespoons (20 g) superfine (caster) sugar

For the cocoa glaze

●

⅓ cup (100 g) neutral glaze

2 tablespoons (10 g) unsweetened cocoa powder

256

FOR THE CHOCOLATE GANACHE

The previous day, heat half the cream in a saucepan. Pour it over the chopped chocolate and gelatin mass. Incorporate the coffee powder using an immersion (stick) blender until the ganache is smooth. Filter through a conical sieve and refrigerate for about 12 hours.

FOR THE CHOCOLATE TART SHELL

Make the chocolate tart shell (case) as described on page 342.

FOR THE COCOA NIB PRALINE

Roast the hazelnuts in the oven at 325°F (165°C/Gas Mark 3) for 15 minutes. Make a dry caramel with the superfine sugar and let cool before processing to a paste. Blend the hazelnuts with the cocoa nibs and oil. In a stand mixer fitted with a flat beater, combine the caramel paste, hazelnut and cocoa nib mixture, and the salt and mix thoroughly.

FOR THE CHOCOLATE-CARAMEL SAUCE

In a saucepan, heat the superfine sugar and ¼ cup (55 g) of the glucose to 365°F (185°C) and cook to an amber caramel. In the meantime, heat 3½ tablespoons (50 g) of the milk with the cream, the remaining glucose, and the fleur de sel. Deglaze the caramel with the hot milk mixture. Cook until the temperature reaches 220°F (105°C), then filter through a conical sieve. When the temperature of the caramel falls to 160°F (70°C), add the butter, chopped chocolate, and remaining milk. Incorporate using an immersion blender and filter through a conical sieve.

FOR THE CHOCOLATE SPONGE CAKE

Preheat the oven to 350°F (175°C/Gas Mark 4). Mix the ground almonds, brown sugar, flour, baking powder, cocoa, and salt with two-thirds (1½ tablespoons/25 g) of an egg white, the yolks, and the cream. Add the melted butter. Beat the remaining egg whites until stiff with the superfine sugar. Fold the beaten egg whites into the batter. Put a 7-inch (18-cm)-diameter pastry ring onto a baking sheet lined with a Silpat mat and pipe in the batter. Bake for 8 minutes, turning the baking sheet around halfway through baking.

FOR ASSEMBLY

Spread a layer of praline inside the tart shell. Insert the sponge disk and cover with a layer of caramel sauce. Refrigerate.

FOR THE COCOA GLAZE

In a saucepan, combine the neutral glaze with the cocoa powder and bring to a boil while stirring with a whisk. Flock the tart immediately with the boiling glaze as described below.

FOR FINISHING

Whip the ganache with a hand mixer. Hold a small (three-pronged) metal stand in one hand. Hold the pastry (piping) bag fitted with a size 104 Saint-Honoré tip (nozzle) in your other hand. Pipe a tight ring of whipped ganache to form the heart of a rose, then pipe semicircular petals all around it, gradually increasing in size. Use a spray gun to uniformly flock the tart with the glaze.

FINGER

LIME

For the lemon ganache

See page 340

For the white chocolate coating

●

½ cup (100 g) cocoa butter

3½ ounces (100 g) white chocolate,
chopped

For finishing

●

6-8 finger lime caviar (pearls)

For the limoncello gel

●

1¼ cups (300 g) limoncello

2½ tablespoons (30 g) superfine
(caster) sugar

1⅞ teaspoons (5 g) agar powder

⅜ teaspoon (1 g) xanthan gum

3 tablespoons (55 g) finger lime
caviar (pearls)

1 cup (170 g) very finely diced
candied lemon peel

2 teaspoons (10 g) coarsely chopped
lemon suprêmes

2 teaspoons (10 g) coarsely chopped
lime suprêmes

2 teaspoons (10 g) coarsely chopped
grapefruit suprêmes

1 tablespoon (10 g) coarsely
chopped orange suprêmes

FOR THE LEMON GANACHE

Make the lemon ganache as described on page 340.

FOR THE LIMONCELLO GEL

In a saucepan, bring the limoncello to a boil, then mix together the
sugar and agar powder and add to the limoncello. Let cool, then mix
with an immersion (stick) blender. Loosen it well, then incorporate the
xanthan gum. Set aside some of this gel for later. Mix the rest with the
finger lime caviar, very finely chopped candied lemon, and coarsely chopped
lemon, lime, grapefruit, and orange suprêmes. Divide the gel into 2¼-inch
(5.5-cm)-diameter hemispherical silicone molds. Freeze for about 3 hours,
then carefully unmold.

FOR THE WHITE CHOCOLATE COATING

Melt and pour the cocoa butter over the chopped white chocolate. Incorporate
using an immersion (stick) blender until smooth. Dip the frozen inserts
into the coating at 95°F (35°C) and drain off the excess.

FOR FINISHING

Pour the reserved gel over the top of each hemisphere to form a small disk.
Whip the ganache with a hand mixer. Use a pastry (piping) bag fitted with
a ⁵/₁₆-inch (8-mm) plain tip (nozzle) to pipe small ganache balls over the
inserts. The aim is to pipe uniform balls around the gel disk, starting at
the top and working your way down. Fill each center with finger lime caviar
(pearls). Refrigerate for about 4 hours before serving.

BANANA

For the sweet tart shell

●

See page 342

For the almond cream

●

See page 336

For the vanilla pastry cream

●

¾ cup (185 g) milk
2 tablespoons (30 g) whipping cream
1 vanilla bean (pod)

3 extra-large (UK large/60 g) egg yolks
¼ cup (50 g) superfine (caster) sugar
2½ tablespoons (15 g) custard powder
1½ tablespoons (20 g) unsalted butter
3 tablespoons (40 g) mascarpone cheese

For the banana gel

●

1 cup (250 g) banana puree
1 teaspoon (2.5 g) xanthan gum

For assembly

●

4 bananas
½ cup (100 g) neutral glaze
½ teaspoon (1 g) vanilla pearls (or vanilla seeds)

FOR THE SWEET TART SHELL

Make the tart shell (case) as described on page 342.

FOR THE ALMOND CREAM

Make the almond cream as described on page 336.

FOR THE VANILLA PASTRY CREAM

Make the vanilla pastry cream as described on page 336.

FOR THE BANANA GEL

Combine the puree with the xanthan gum and incorporate using an immersion (stick) blender.

FOR ASSEMBLY

Preheat the oven to 340°F (170°C/Gas Mark 3½). Fill the tart shell with almond and vanilla cream and bake for 8 minutes. Let cool for about 15 minutes. Pipe a ball of pastry cream at the center of the tart to serve as a reference point. Pipe a ball of pastry cream at the edge of the tart and continue inward to make a strip reaching the ball at the center. Repeat the process with the banana gel. Cover the entire tart with alternating strips. Peel the bananas. Dice half a banana and distribute the pieces evenly over the tart. Smooth with a spatula (palette knife). Cut the remaining bananas into thin slices and arrange over the tart in a rosette pattern. In a saucepan, combine the neutral glaze with the vanilla pearls and bring to a boil. Transfer to a spray gun and flock the tart (or brush the tart lightly with the glaze).

COCONUT AND PASSiON FRUiT

For the sweet tart shell

See page 342

For the coconut praline

½ cup (85 g) almonds

3¾ cups (270 g) shredded coconut

¾ cupu (150 g) superfine (caster) sugar

½ teaspoon (2 g) fleur de sel

For the passion fruit crémeux

½ cup plus 1 tablespoon (140 g) passion fruit puree

2½ teaspoons (5 g) peeled and grated fresh ginger

3 extra-large (UK large/160 g) eggs

2¼ teaspoons (15 g) honey

¾ cup (1½ sticks/165 g) unsalted butter

3¼ teaspoons (18 g) gelatin mass (¾ teaspoon/2.5 g gelatin powder hydrated in 3¼ teaspoons/15.5 g water)

For the coconut gel

⅓ cup plus 1 tablespoon (100 g) coconut puree

⅜ teaspoon (1 g) xanthan gum

For the passion fruit gel

1½ cups (370 g) passion fruit puree

1½ cups (20 g) superfine (caster) sugar

2⅝ teaspoons (7 g) agar powder

1⅛ teaspoons (3 g) xanthan gum

3 passion fruits

For the meringue

See page 341

For finishing

Shredded coconut

Non-melting snow white topping sugar, such as Codineige or King Arthur

264

FOR THE SWEET TART SHELL

Make the tart shell (case) as described on page 342.

FOR THE COCONUT PRALINE

Make the coconut praline as described on page 342.

FOR THE PASSION FRUIT CRÉMEUX

In a saucepan, combine the passion fruit puree with the grated ginger and bring to a boil. Mix together with the eggs and honey and pour into the pan. Heat to 220°F (105°C), then incorporate the butter and gelatin mass.

FOR THE COCONUT GEL

Mix the coconut puree with the xanthan gum.

FOR THE PASSION FRUIT GEL

In a saucepan, bring the passion fruit puree to a boil, then add the superfine sugar, the agar, and xanthan gum. Incorporate using an immersion (stick) blender and refrigerate until set. Blend again. Cut open the passion fruits and collect the seeds and juice. Lightly process the seeds in a little water using an immersion blender to make them less viscous. Drain, then mix the passion fruit juice and seeds into the blended gel.

FOR THE MERINGUE

Make the meringue as described on page 341.

FOR ASSEMBLY

Spread a 1/16-inch (2-mm)-thick layer of coconut praline over the bottom of the tart shell. Freeze for about 30 minutes. Cover with a layer of passion fruit gel twice the thickness of the praline. Return to the freezer for about 1 hour. Fill the tart to the top with a layer of passion fruit crémeux and smooth with a spatula (palette knife). Freeze until set.

FOR FINISHING

Preheat the oven to 325°F (165°C/Gas Mark 3). Over the well-frozen crémeux, pipe rings of "broken balls" with the meringue. To do so, use a pastry (piping) bag fitted with a size 14 plain tip (nozzle). After piping a ball, make a short upward, then downward stroke, as if breaking off but without prolonging the movement. Pipe the following ball next to the first and continue in this way around the tart. Repeat the process two or three times to make rings with increasingly reduced diameters, always staggering the placement of the first ball. Sprinkle the entire surface with shredded coconut, then lightly dust with snow sugar. Bake for 16 minutes and let cool. Finish by filling the center of the tart with coconut gel to make the heart.

MCHA

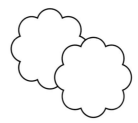

For the coffee dacquoise

2½ large (UK medium/80 g) egg whites (⅓ cup)

3 tablespoons (35 g) superfine (caster) sugar

¾ cup (70 g) ground almonds

2 tablespoons (15 g) all-purpose (plain) flour

⅓ cup plus 2 tablespoons (55 g) confectioners' (icing) sugar

¼ cup (12 g) instant coffee powder

For the milk chocolate coating

See page 338

For the hazelnut praline

See page 342

For the coffee-flavored Paris-Brest cream

½ cup plus 1 tablespoon (140 g) milk

¼ cup (60 g) whipping cream

1 teaspoon (2 g) vanilla pearls (or vanilla seeds)

For the coffee crisp

See page 337

For the coffee crémeux

See page 336

2 large (UK medium/35 g) egg yolks

3 tablespoons (35 g) superfine (caster) sugar

1¾ teaspoons (10 g) custard powder

4 teaspoons (10 g) all-purpose (plain) flour

4 tablespoons (60 g) unsalted butter

1 tablespoon (12 g) cocoa butter

5 teaspoons (28 g) gelatin mass (1¼ teaspoons/4 g gelatin powder hydrated in 5 teaspoons/24 g water)

2½ teaspoons (12 g) mascarpone cheese

½ cup (110 g) coffee paste

For the coffee praline

1 cup (150 g) almonds

3½ cups (250 g) coffee beans

⅓ cup (75 g) superfine (caster) sugar

¾ teaspoon (3 g) fleur de sel

2 tablespoons (40 g) hazelnut praline

½ cup (120 g) whipped cream

269

FOR THE COFFEE DACQUOISE

Preheat the oven to 340°F (170°C/Gas Mark 3½). Make a French meringue by beating the egg whites until stiff, incorporating the superfine sugar in three batches. The meringue is ready when it forms a peak on the end of the whisk without collapsing. Fold in the ground almonds, flour, confectioners' sugar, and coffee powder. Pipe the dacquoise batter into a 5½-inch (14-cm)-diameter pastry ring and bake for 16 minutes.

FOR THE COFFEE CRISP

Make the coffee crisp as described on page 337.

FOR THE COFFEE CRÉMEUX

Make the coffee crémeux as described on page 336.

FOR THE COFFEE PRALINE

Roast the almonds and coffee beans in the oven at 325°F (165°C/Gas Mark 3) for 15 minutes. In a saucepan, heat 1½ tablespoons (25 g) water with the superfine sugar to 230°F (110°C), then add the roasted almonds and coffee beans. Coat well in the syrup and let caramelize, stirring constantly. Transfer to a Silpat mat. Let cool, then transfer to a food processor, add the fleur de sel, and process to a paste.

FOR THE MILK CHOCOLATE COATING

Make the milk chocolate coating as described on page 338.

Make the hazelnut praline as described on page 342.

FOR THE COFFEE-FLAVORED PARIS-BREST CREAM

In a saucepan, combine the milk and cream with the vanilla pearls and bring to a boil. In the meantime, using a whisk, beat the yolks in a large bowl with the superfine sugar, custard powder, and flour until thick and pale. Pour the boiling mixture over the yolk mixture. Let boil for 2 minutes while stirring. Incorporate the butter, cocoa butter, gelatin mass, mascarpone, coffee paste, and praline. Refrigerate for about 4 hours. In a stand mixer fitted with a whisk attachment, smooth the cream, then add the whipped cream.

FOR THE INSERT

Spread a layer of the crisp inside a 6¼-inch (16-cm)-diameter pastry ring. Place the dacquoise disk on top. Fill and cover with coffee crémeux, making sure the insert does not exceed a thickness of ¾ inch (2 cm). Freeze for about 3 hours.

FOR ASSEMBLY

Whip the Paris-Brest cream with a hand mixer. Pipe cream over the entire surface of a 7-inch (18-cm)-diameter Pavoni silicone entremets mold. Pipe more in the middle so the insert will be well centered. Add a thin layer of praline. Introduce the frozen insert. Fill to the top with Paris-Brest cream and smooth with a spatula (palette knife). Freeze for about 3 hours.

FOR FINISHING

Use a pastry (piping) bag fitted with a small star tip (nozzle) to pipe a ball of Paris-Brest cream in the center of the entremets. Pipe the cream in concentric rings to cover the entire surface. Freeze for about 2 hours. Use a 3¼-inch (8-cm)-diameter cookie cutter to make a hole in the center. Use a spray gun to cover the entremets uniformly with milk chocolate coating. Pour a thin layer of coffee praline into the center. Refrigerate for about 4 hours before serving.

GALETTE

For the frangipane

½ cup plus 1 tablespoon (140 g) milk

1½ tablespoons (25 g) whipping cream

1 vanilla bean (pod), split and scraped

1 medium (UK small/45 g) egg

3½ tablespoons (40 g) superfine (caster) sugar

2 teaspoons (12 g) custard powder

1 tablespoon (15 g) unsalted butter

2 tablespoons (30 g) mascarpone cheese

For the almond-hazelnut paste

14 tablespoons (120 g) whole almonds

14 tablespoons (120 g) whole hazelnuts

2 tablespoons plus 1 teaspoon (18 g) confectioners' (icing) sugar

1½ teaspoons (6 g) fleur de sel

For the insert

4 tablespoons (60 g) unsalted butter

¼ cup plus 1 tablespoon (60 g) superfine (caster) sugar

⅔ cup (60 g) ground almonds

1 tablespoon (10 g) potato starch

1 jumbo (UK large/60 g) egg

1½ tablespoons (25 g) vanilla pastry cream

2 tablespoons (25 g) almond-hazelnut paste

For the flaky brioche

½ cup (125 g) milk

⅞ small cake (15 g) fresh yeast, or 2⅞ teaspoons active dry (easy-blend) yeast, dissolved in milk or water

2½ cups (340 g) bread (strong) flour

⅞ teaspoon (5 g) salt

1½ tablespoons (20 g) superfine (caster) sugar

1 jumbo (UK large/60 g) egg

2 tablespoons (30 g) unsalted butter, softened

1⅓ cups (300 g) unsalted dry butter (84% fat content)

For assembly

1 egg

Unsalted butter

Superfine (caster) sugar

FOR THE FRANGIPANE

In a saucepan, combine the milk with the cream and bring to a boil. Add the split and scraped vanilla bean and seeds, then remove from the heat. Cover and let infuse for about 10 minutes. Bring back to a boil and filter through a conical sieve. In the meantime, using a whisk, beat the eggs in a large bowl with the sugar and custard powder until thick and pale. Add them to the boiling mixture and let boil for 2 minutes before incorporating the butter and mascarpone.

FOR THE ALMOND-HAZELNUT PASTE

Preheat the oven to 330°F (165°C). Toast the almonds and hazelnuts for 15 to 20 minutes, then blend them in a food processor, adding the confectioners'sugar and fleur de sel.

FOR THE INSERT

In a stand mixer fitted with flat beater attachment, cream the butter with the sugar, ground almonds, and starch. Gradually add the eggs. Finish with the frangipane and nut paste. Put the mixture into a 5½-inch (14-cm)-diameter and 1-inch 2.5-cm-deep pastry ring. Freeze.

FOR THE FLAKY BRIOCHE

In a stand mixer fitted with a dough hook, combine the milk, yeast, flour, salt, and sugar, and mix on speed 1 while gradually adding the eggs. Increase to speed 2 and continue mixing until the dough pulls away from the sides. Cut the softened butter into cubes, add to the dough, and knead until smooth. Let the dough rise at room temperature (68-77°F/20-25 °C) for about 1 hour. Use your palms to flatten and deflate the dough, then roll out into a rectangle. Shape the dry butter into a rectangle half the size and place it in the center of the dough. Fold over the sides of the dough to encase the butter and roll out, then fold with a simple turn (letter fold). Refrigerate for about 30 minutes. Cut out ten ⅜-inch (5-mm)-wide strips from the dough. Roll out the remaining dough and cut out two 8-inch (20-cm)-diameter disks. Lay the ten strips flat over one of the disks. Cover with parchment (baking) paper and roll out the strips with a rolling pin. Refrigerate.

FOR ASSEMBLY

Preheat the oven to 350°F (175°C/Gas Mark 4). Place the frozen insert at the center of the brioche disk covered with the strips. Cover with the other disk and press to remove any air bubbles. Seal the edges of the dough by crimping with a fork. Use a 7-inch (18-cm)-diameter flower-shape pastry ring to cut the brioche-covered insert into a flower shape. Brush the flat part with beaten egg. Grease the flower-shape pastry ring with butter and place on parchment paper, also greased with butter and sugar. Introduce the assembled galette, with the brioche strips facing downward. Bake for 35 minutes. When it comes out of the oven, turn the galette over and carefully unmold.

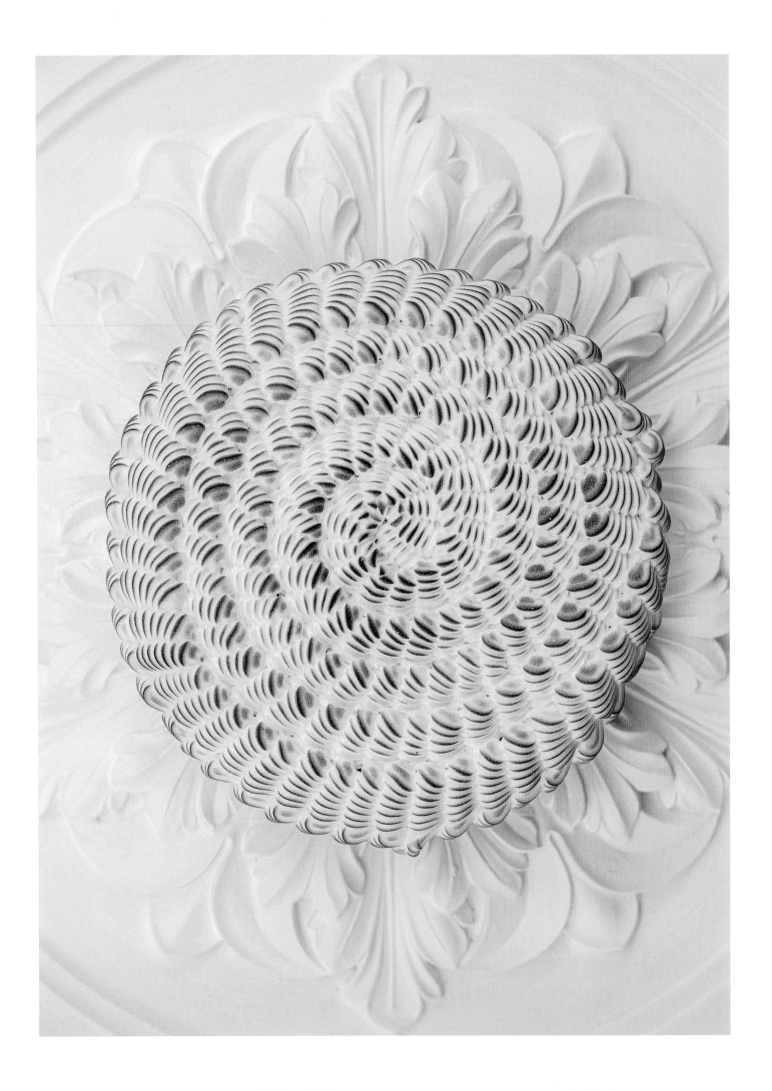

BAKD ALASKA

For the Tahitian vanilla ice cream

2¼ cups (550 g) milk

½ cup plus 1 tablespoon (130 g) whipping cream

3 Tahitian vanilla beans (pods), split and scraped

½ cup plus 1 tablespoon (40 g) instant dry milk powder

3 tablespoons (40 g) glucose powder

1 teaspoon (5 g) stabilizer (super neutrose)

4 large (UK medium/70 g) egg yolks

¾ cup (140 g) superfine (caster) sugar

For the Madagascar vanilla ice cream

2¼ cups (550 g) milk

½ cup plus 1 tablespoon (130 g) whipping cream

3 Madagascar (bourbon) vanilla beans (pods) split and scraped

½ cup plus 1 tablespoon (40 g) instant dry milk powder

3 tablespoons (40 g) glucose powder

1 teaspoon (5 g) stabilizer (super neutrose)

4 large (UK medium/70 g) egg yolks

¾ cup (140 g) superfine (caster) sugar

For the Italian meringue

1½ cups (300 g) superfine (caster) sugar

6 extra-large (UK large/220 g) egg whites

For the Joconde cake

3 large (UK medium/140 g) eggs

⅞ cup (105 g) confectioners' (icing) sugar

1⅛ cups (105 g) ground almonds

¼ cup (30 g) all-purpose (plain) flour

1½ tablespoons (20 g) unsalted butter

2¾ large (UK medium/90 g) egg whites (⅜ cup)

3¾ teaspoons (15 g) superfine (caster) sugar

2½ tablespoons (40 g) rum

For the vanilla praline

1 cup (150 g) almonds

1 vanilla bean (pod)

½ cup (100 g) superfine (caster) sugar

FOR THE TAHITIAN VANILLA ICE CREAM

In a saucepan, heat the milk and cream with the vanilla beans (pods) and seeds to about 120°F (50°C). Add the milk powder, glucose, and stabilizer. Bring to a boil and remove the beans. Using a whisk, beat the yolks with the superfine sugar until thick and pale. Then add the yolk and sugar mixture. Cook until thick enough to coat a spoon. Let age for about 12 hours before churning.

FOR THE MADAGASCAR VANILLA ICE CREAM

In a saucepan, heat the milk and cream with the vanilla beans and seeds to about 120°F (50°C). Add the milk powder, glucose, and stabilizer. Bring to a boil and remove the beans. Using a whisk, beat the yolks with the superfine sugar until thick and pale. Then add the yoke and sugar mixture. Cook until thick enough to coat a spoon. Let age for about 12 hours before churning.

FOR THE ITALIAN MERINGUE

In a saucepan, heat ¼ cup plus 2 teaspoons (70 g) water with the superfine sugar to 250°F (121°C). When the mixture reaches about 240°F (115°C), beat the egg whites until they are stiff. Gradually add the syrup to make the Italian meringue.

FOR THE JOCONDE CAKE

Preheat the oven to 350°F (175°C/Gas Mark 4). In a stand mixer fitted with a whisk attachment, beat the eggs with the confectioners' (icing) sugar and ground almonds. Incorporate the flour and melted butter. Beat the egg whites until stiff with the superfine (caster) sugar. Fold the beaten egg whites into the batter. Spread the batter over a baking sheet lined with a Silpat mat. Bake for 10 minutes. Let cool, cut into a 6¼-inch (16-cm)-diameter disk, and brush with rum to soak.

FOR THE VANILLA PRALINE

Roast the almonds and vanilla bean in the oven at 325°F (165°C/Gas Mark 3) for 15 minutes. In a saucepan, heat the superfine sugar and ¼ cup plus 2 teaspoons (70 g) water to 230°F (110°C). Add the almonds and vanilla bean, stir to coat well in the syrup, and let caramelize. Cool the caramel completely before blending in a food processor to form a paste.

FOR ASSEMBLY

Place a 6¼-inch (16-cm)-diameter pastry ring on a serving dish. Make a layer of Tahitian vanilla ice cream, top with the joconde cake disk, and add a layer of Madagascar vanilla ice cream. Cover everything with vanilla praline. Freeze for about 1 hour, until set.

FOR FINISHING

Carefully lift off the pastry ring. Use a pastry (piping) bag fitted with a large size star tip (nozzle) to pipe the meringue in the shape of snail shells. Start in the center and cover the entire surface of the cake. Use a chef's torch to brown the meringue and serve immediately.

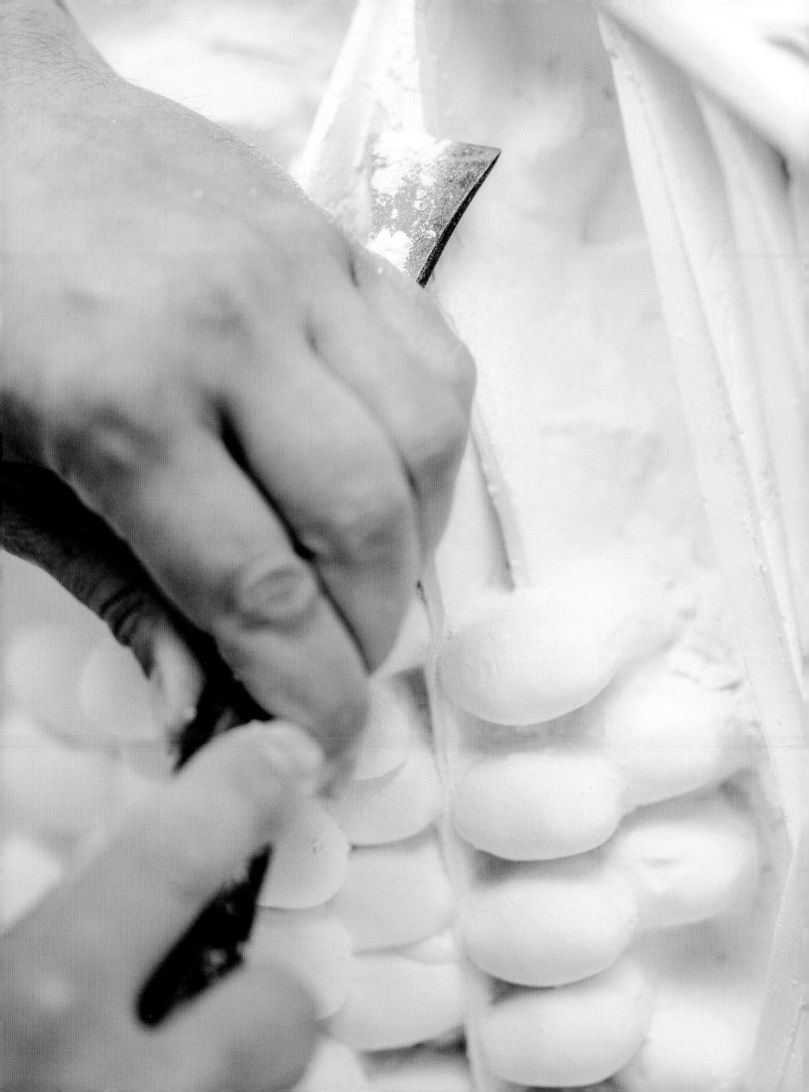

COOKiES

PEANUT

For the cookie dough

●

½ cup plus 3 tablespoons
(1⅜ sticks/160 g) unsalted butter

⅞ cup (200 g) packed brown sugar

3½ tablespoons (40 g) piloncillo
(or superfine/caster) sugar

3½ tablespoons (40 g) superfine
(caster) sugar

2 teaspoons (8 g) fleur de sel

3¾ teaspoons (20 g) peanut butter

¾ teaspoon (3 g) baking soda

2½ cups (320 g) all-purpose (plain)
flour

1½ large (UK medium/75 g) eggs
(⅓ cup)

⅔ cup (100 g) chopped peanuts

For the peanut praline

●

2⅔ cups (380 g) peanuts

½ cup plus 1 tablespoon (115 g)
superfine (caster) sugar

2 teaspoons (8 g) fleur de sel

For the caramel sauce

●

See page 335

For the caramelized peanuts

●

2¾ cups (400 g) peanuts

⅔ cup (120 g) superfine (caster)
sugar

A pinch of tartaric acid

CHOCOLATE-VANILLA

For the cookie dough

●

7 tablespoons (100 g) unsalted
butter

½ cup (100 g) packed brown sugar

¼ cup (50 g) superfine (caster)
sugar

⅔ cup (125 g) piloncillo (or
superfine/caster) sugar

2 tablespoons (25 g) vanilla paste

1 large (UK medium/50 g) egg

1¼ teaspoons (5 g) fleur de sel

½ teaspoons (2 g) baking soda

1⅔ cups 200 g all-purpose (plain)
flour

1 cup (170 g) semisweet (dark)
chocolate chips

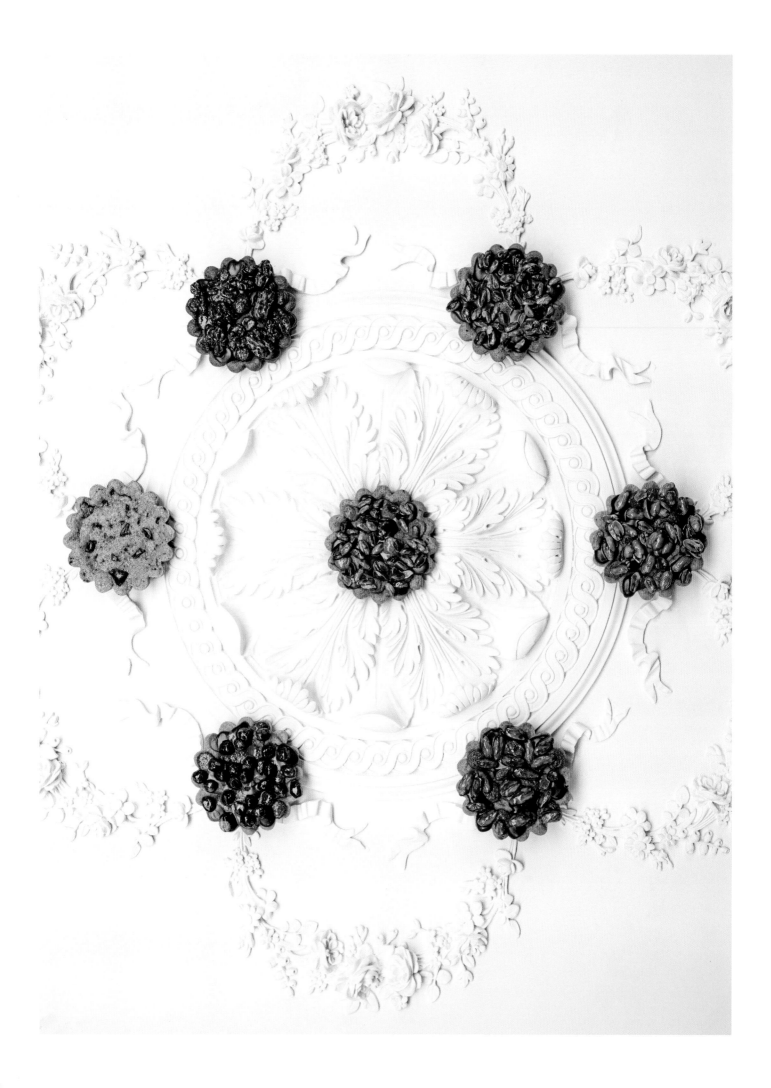

FOR THE COOKIE DOUGH

In a stand mixer fitted with a flat beater, cream the butter with the sugars, peanut butter, and baking soda. Add the flour and eggs. Finish by incorporating the chopped peanuts.

FOR THE PEANUT PRALINE

Roast the peanuts in the oven at 325°F (165°C/Gas Mark 3) for 15 minutes. Make a dry caramel with the sugar and let cool before pulsing in a food processor to form a paste. Grind the peanuts. In a stand mixer fitted with a flat beater, combine all the ingredients and mix thoroughly.

FOR THE CARAMEL SAUCE

Make the caramel sauce as described on page 335.

FOR THE CARAMELIZED PEANUTS

Roast the peanuts in the oven at 340°F (170°C/Gas Mark 3½) for 15 minutes. Make a dark caramel with the sugar, 3½ tablespoons (50 g) water, and the tartaric acid. Add the peanuts. Let caramelize for a few minutes, then transfer to a baking sheet lined with a Silpat mat or parchment (baking) paper. Space the peanuts apart to prevent them from sticking together.

FOR ASSEMBLY

Preheat the oven to 325°F (165°C/Gas Mark 3). Shape the dough into ten 3½-ounce (100-g) balls. Place them on a baking sheet lined with a Silpat mat (or parchment/baking paper). Bake for about 7 minutes. When the cookies come out of the oven, pipe three dots of praline and three dots of caramel on top of them. Finish by covering them with a random arrangement of caramelized peanuts.

For a wider range of flavors, you can replace the peanuts (in the nut butter, praline, and caramelized nuts) with pecans, pistachios, hazelnuts, or almonds.

CHOCOLATE-VANILLA

FOR THE COOKIE DOUGH

Preheat the oven to 325°F (165°C/Gas Mark 3). In a stand mixer fitted with a flat beater attachment, cream the butter with the sugars and vanilla paste. Add the eggs, previously mixed with the salt and baking soda, then the flour. Finish with the chocolate chips. Shape the dough into ten 3½-ounces (100-g) balls. Arrange on a baking sheet lined with a Silpat mat (or parchment/baking paper) for 7 minutes.

MARBLE

For the chocolate ganache

1 ⅓ cups plus 1½ tablespoons (340 g) whipping cream

9½ ounces (270 g) Alain Ducasse dark chocolate, chopped

¼ cup plus 2 teaspoons (100 g) honey

7 tablespoons (100 g) unsalted butter

For the chocolate cake batter

½ cup (65 g) all-purpose (plain) flour

⅞ teaspoon (4 g) baking powder

2½ tablespoons (13 g) unsweetened cocoa powder

2½ large (UK medium/130 g) eggs (½ cup)

3½ tablespoons (40 g) trimoline (inverted sugar)

⅓ cup (65 g) superfine (caster) sugar

⅓ cup plus 1½ tablespoons (40 g) ground almonds

2½ tablespoons (40 g) whipping cream

3 tablespoons (40 g) grapeseed oil

1 ounce (25 g) bittersweet (dark) chocolate (70% cocoa), melted

For the vanilla cake batter

2½ large (UK medium/130 g) eggs (½ cup)

3½ tablespoons (40 g) trimoline (inverted sugar)

⅓ cup (65 g) superfine (caster) sugar

⅓ cup plus 1½ tablespoons (40 g) ground almonds

½ cup plus 1½ tablespoons (75 g) all-purpose (plain) flour

1 teaspoon (5 g) baking powder

¼ cup (65 g) whipping cream

1 vanilla bean (pod)

2½ tablespoons (15 g) vanilla pearls (or vanilla seeds)

3 tablespoons (40 g) grapeseed oil

1 ounce (25 g) white chocolate, melted

For the dark chocolate coating

½ cup (100 g) unsweetened cocoa butter

3½ ounces (100 g) semisweet (dark) chocolate, chopped

FOR THE CHOCOLATE GANACHE

The previous day, bring half the cream to a boil in a saucepan. Pour the hot cream over the chopped chocolate, honey, and butter. Incorporate using an immersion (stick) blender, adding the remaining cream, until the ganache is smooth. Filter through a conical sieve and refrigerate for about 12 hours.

FOR THE CHOCOLATE CAKE BATTER

Mix and sift the flour, baking powder, and cocoa powder. In a stand mixer fitted with a flat beater attachment, beat the eggs with the trimoline, sugar, and ground almonds. Add the flour mixture, before incorporating the cream at room temperature. Add the grapeseed oil and melted chocolate to half of the mixture, then mix everything together.

FOR THE VANILLA CAKE BATTER

Mix and sift the flour and baking powder. In a stand mixer fitted with a flat beater attachment, beat the eggs with the trimoline, sugar, and ground almonds. Add the flour and baking powder mixture before incorporating the cream at room temperature, split and scraped vanilla bean and seeds, and vanilla pearls. Mix well, then remove the vanilla bean. Add the grapeseed oil and melted chocolate to half of the mixture, then mix everything together.

ASSEMBLY

Preheat the oven to 350°F (175°C/Gas Mark 4). Pour the vanilla cake batter into a 5½-inch (14-cm)-diameter pastry ring, then add the chocolate batter and use a fork to create a marbled effect. Bake at 350°F (180°C/Gas Mark 4) for 20 minutes, then at 325°F (160°C/Gas Mark 3) for 25 minutes. Let cool.

FOR THE DARK CHOCOLATE COATING

Melt and pour the cocoa butter over the chopped dark chocolate.

FOR FiNiSHiNG

Whip the ganache with a hand mixer.

Step 1
Use a pastry (piping) bag fitted with a size 14 basketweave tip (nozzle), pipe the ganache all around the cake. Start at the top and work your way downward for an even draped effect. Flick your wrist slightly backward to make a circular shape at the top of the cake.

Step 2
For the rose at the center of the cake, pipe a tight ring of whipped ganache to form the heart, then pipe semicircular petals all around it, gradually increasing them in size. Use a spray gun to uniformly flock the cake with the dark chocolate coating.

SAVOY

CAKE

For the batter

●

6½ extra-large (UK large/240 g) egg whites (1 cup)

1 cup (200 g) superfine (caster) sugar

4¼ extra-large (UK large/80 g) egg yolks (⅓ cup)

1⅞ cups (230 g) all-purpose (plain) flour, plus more for dusting the pans

Unsalted butter, for greasing

Preheat the oven to 325°F (165°C/Gas Mark 3). Beat the egg whites while gradually adding the sugar until stiff. Using a silicone spatula (palette knife), first fold in the yolks, followed by the flour. To prepare the flower-shape baking pans, brush two times with melted butter, then sprinkle with flour and tap to remove excess. Pour one-sixth (4⅜ ounces/125 g) of the batter into each baking pan. Bake for 12 minutes.

CHEESECAKE

For the shortbread crust

¾ cup (1½ sticks/165 g) unsalted butter

1 teaspoon (6 g) salt

⅓ cup (75 g) packed brown sugar

1¾ cups (220 g) all-purpose (plain) flour

scant ½ cup (2 g) baking powder

¼ cup (40 g) potato starch

For the cream cheese mousse

⅞ cup (200 g) whipping cream

5 large (UK medium/85 g) egg yolks

3½ tablespoons (40 g) superfine (caster) sugar

1 tablespoon (17 g) gelatin mass (¾ teaspoon/2.5 g gelatin powder hydrated in 1 tablespoon/14.5 g water)

1⅜ cups (330 g) mascarpone cheese

⅔ cup (150 g) cream cheese, such as Philadelphia

For the strawberry preserves

3 cups (475 g) fully ripe strawberries

¼ cup plus 2 teaspoons (70 g) strawberry juice

¾ cup (145 g) superfine (caster) sugar

¼ cup (50 g) glucose powder

2½ teaspoons (10 g) pectin NH

½ teaspoon (3 g) tartaric acid

For the white chocolate coating

See page 338

FOR THE SHORTBREAD CRUST

Preheat the oven to 300°F (150°C/Gas Mark 2). In a stand mixer fitted with a flat beater attachment, combine the butter, salt, brown sugar, flour, baking powder, and potato starch and mix to a smooth dough. Spread the dough in a ⅜-inch (1-cm) thickness over a baking sheet lined with a Silpat mat. Bake for about 20 minutes. Use a 6¼-inch (16-cm)-diameter pastry ring to cut out a shortbread disk for the crust (base).

FOR THE CREAM CHEESE MOUSSE

In a saucepan, bring the cream to a boil. Beat the yolks with the superfine sugar. Pour a little boiling cream over this mixture, then return it to the saucepan to make a crème anglaise. Cook for 2 minutes, then incorporate the gelatin mass using an immersion (stick) blender. Filter through a conical sieve, then add the mascarpone and cream cheese and blend until a mousse-like consistency is achieved. Refrigerate for about 6 hours.

FOR THE STRAWBERRY PRESERVES

Make a preserve by cooking the strawberries for about 30 minutes, gradually adding the juice. Add the superfine sugar, glucose powder, pectin, and tartaric acid, mix, and bring to a boil for 1 minute. Refrigerate until set.

FOR THE WHITE CHOCOLATE COATING

Make the white chocolate coating as described on page 338.

FOR ASSEMBLY

Whip the cream cheese mousse with a hand mixer. Pipe a thin bed of mousse inside a 6¼-inch (16-cm)-diameter pastry ring. Cover with a layer of strawberry preserves. The insert should not exceed a thickness of ¾ inch (2 cm). Freeze. Pipe the cream cheese mousse over the entire surface of a 7-inch (18-cm)-diameter Pavoni silicone entremets mold. Pipe more in the middle so the insert will be well centered. Add the insert and cover with mousse. Smooth with a spatula (palette knife). Freeze for about 6 hours, until set. Carefully unmold the cake.

FOR FINISHING

Use a pastry (piping) bag fitted with a size 104 Saint-Honoré tip (nozzle) to pipe plenty of small upright petals of cream cheese mousse over the cake. Start at the center and work your way outward, staggering the petals by starting each one in the middle of the preceding one. The petals should increasingly open out as you progress, giving the illusion of a flower. Use a spray gun to uniformly flock the cake with the white chocolate coating.

CARAMEL

For the almond crisp

3½ cups (500 g) whole almonds

⅔ cup (130 g) superfine (caster) sugar

¼ cup (50 g) cocoa butter, melted

2 cups (100 g) feuilletine flakes

½ teaspoon (2 g) fleur de sel

For the caramel sauce

Double the ingredients on page 335.

For the caramel glaze

½ cup (115 g) milk

1 cup (235 g) whipping cream

⅓ cup (75 g) glucose powder

1 vanilla bean (pod), split and scraped

1½ cups (295 g) superfine (caster) sugar

2 tablespoons (20 g) potato starch

3½ tablespoons (56 g) gelatin mass (2½ teaspoons/8 g gelatin powder hydrated in 3½ tablespoons/48 g water)

For the ladyfinger sponge cake

5 large (UK medium/85 g) egg yolks

½ cup plus 1½ tablespoons (120 g) superfine (caster) sugar

5⅓ large (UK medium/175 g egg whites (¾ cup)

1 cup (120 g) all-purpose (plain) flour, sifted

Superfine (caster) sugar

Confectioners' (icing) sugar

For the vanilla and caramel ganache

1 cup (225 g) whipping cream

5 large (UK medium/85 g) egg yolks

5½ tablespoons (65 g) superfine (caster) sugar

1 tablespoon (17 g) gelatin mass (¾ teaspoon/2.5 g gelatin powder hydrated in 1 tablespoon/14.5 g water)

1⅓ cups plus 1½ tablespoons (330 g) mascarpone cheese

2½ teaspoons (5 g) vanilla pearls (or vanilla seeds)

For the milk chocolate coating

Make the coating as described on page 338.

For the caramel Chantilly cream

¾ cup (150 g) superfine (caster) sugar

3 cups (750 g) whipping cream

FOR THE ALMOND CRISP

Dry the almonds in the oven at 210°F (100°C) for 1 hour. In a saucepan, combine 2½ tablespoons (40 g) water with the superfine sugar and heat to 230°F (110°C). Add the dried almonds and coat well with the syrup. Let cool, then use an immersion (stick) blender to crush and blend the almonds with the melted cocoa butter, feuilletine flakes, and fleur de sel.

FOR THE CARAMEL SAUCE

Make the caramel sauce as described on page 335.

FOR THE CARAMEL GLAZE

In a saucepan, combine the milk and cream with the glucose and split and scraped vanilla bean and seeds. Make a dry caramel with 1 cup plus 2 tablespoons (225 g) of the superfine sugar. Deglaze with the hot cream. Mix together the remaining sugar and the starch and add to the saucepan. Let boil for 2 minutes, then filter through a conical sieve, add the gelatin mass, and incorporate using an immersion blender.

FIRST LAYER ASSEMBLY

Spread the crisp inside a 7-inch (18-cm)-diameter pastry ring. Top with a thin layer of caramel sauce. Transfer to a rack and cover everything with the caramel glaze. Refrigerate until set.

FOR THE LADYFINGER SPONGE CAKE

In a stand mixer fitted with a flat beater attachment, beat the egg yolks with half the sugar. Beat the egg whites until stiff with the remaining sugar. Combine the two mixtures and incorporate the sifted flour. In a 6¼-inch (14-cm)-diameter pastry ring, spread the batter to a ⅜-inch (1-cm) thickness. Dust lightly with superfine sugar and confectioners' sugar. Bake for 5-6 minutes.

FOR THE VANILLA AND CARAMEL GANACHE

In a saucepan, bring ⅜ cup plus 1 tablespoon (100 g) of the cream to a boil. Beat the yolks with the 3½ tablespoons (40 g) of the superfine sugar. Pour a little boiling cream over this mixture, then return it to the saucepan to make a crème anglaise. Cook for 2 minutes, then incorporate the gelatin mass, mascarpone, and ⅜ cup plus 1 tablespoon (100 g) of the cream using an immersion (stick) blender. Filter through a conical sieve. In the meantime, make a dry caramel with the remaining 2 tablespoons (25 g) superfine sugar. Bring the remaining cream to a boil with the vanilla pearls. Deglaze the caramel with the hot cream, then cook again for 1-2 minutes. Add to the previous mixture and incorporate using an immersion blender. Refrigerate for about 12 hours.

FOR THE MILK CHOCOLATE COATING

Make the milk chocolate coating as described on page 338.

FOR THE CARAMEL CHANTILLY CREAM

Make a dry caramel with the superfine sugar. Bring ⅔ cup (150 g) of the cream to a boil. When the caramel reaches 365°F (185°C), deglaze with the hot cream. Incorporate using an immersion (stick) blender, then gradually mix in the remaining cold cream. Blend again and refrigerate for about 4 hours.

SECOND LAYER ASSEMBLY

Unmold the sponge. Whip the ganache with a hand mixer. Spread a thin layer of ganache in a 5½-inch (14-cm)-diameter pastry ring. Place the sponge disk over it and cover with another thin layer of ganache. The total amount of ganache should be equal to that of the sponge and together should not exceed a thickness of ¾ inch (2 cm). Freeze for about 3 hours. Use a pastry (piping) bag fitted with a size 20 Saint-Honoré tip (nozzle) to pipe semicircles of ganache over the top, starting at the edge and moving toward the center. Return to the freezer.

FOR THE INSERT

Pour the remaining caramel sauce into 2¾-inch (7-cm)-diameter hemispherical molds. Freeze for about 2 hours, until set. Join two hemispheres together to form a sphere. Pipe a bed of ganache inside a 3½-inch (9-cm)-diameter pastry ring. Place the insert at the center and fill to the top with ganache, smoothing the surface. Freeze for about 6 hours, until set.

THIRD LEVEL ASSEMBLY

Use a pastry bag fitted with a ⅜-inch (10-mm) plain tip to pipe balls of whipped ganache all around the frozen insert. Cover the center with caramel glaze.

FINAL ASSEMBLY

Use a spray gun to uniformly flock the second level with milk chocolate coating. Place this level on top of the first. Finish by topping with the third level. Refrigerate for about 4 hours before serving.

MONT-BLANC

For the vanilla ganache

2²⁄₃ cups (625 g) whipping cream

1 vanilla bean (pod)

5 ounces (140 g) ivory white couverture chocolate

2 tablespoons (35 g) gelatin mass (1½ teaspoons/5 g gelatin powder hydrated in 2 tablespoons/30 g water)

For the chestnut sponge cake

½ cup plus ½ tablespoon (1 stick plus ½ tablespoon/120 g) unsalted butter

¹⁄₃ cup plus 1½ tablespoons (140 g) chestnut paste

8½ extra-large (UK large/160 g egg yolks (²⁄₃ cup)

1 cup (180 g) superfine (caster) sugar

6½ extra-large (UK large/240 g) egg whites (1 cup)

2 tablespoons (15 g) all-purpose (plain) flour

1½ tablespoons (15 g) potato starch

Candied chestnut pieces

For the chestnut cream

¾ cup (240 g) sweetened condensed milk

2½ cups (600 g) crème de marrons (chestnut spread)

1¾ cups (600 g) chestnut paste

For the meringue

5¼ extra-large (UK large/100 g) egg whites (¹⁄₃ cup plus 1½ tablespoons)

½ cup (100 g) superfine (caster) sugar

¾ cup plus 1 tablespoon (100 g) confectioners' (icing) sugar

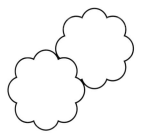

301

FOR THE VANILLA GANACHE

Make the vanilla ganache as described on page 340.

FOR THE CHESTNUT CREAM

In a copper saucepan, caramelize the condensed milk in the oven at 195°F (90°C) for 4 hours. Let cool, then transfer to a food processor. Add the chestnut spread and paste with ½ cup (120 g) water and blend until the mixture thickens. Refrigerate for about 12 hours.

FOR THE MERINGUE

Preheat the oven to 195°F (90°C). Beat the egg whites until stiff, adding the superfine sugar in three batches. The meringue is ready when it forms a peak on the end of the whisk without collapsing. Sift the confectioners' sugar. Pipe the meringue in a swirl inside a 7-inch (18-cm)-diameter pastry ring placed on a baking sheet covered with a Silpat mat. Bake for about 1 hour–1 hour 30 minutes.

FOR THE CHESTNUT SPONGE CAKE

Preheat the oven to 350°F (175°C/Gas Mark 4). In a stand mixer fitted with a flat beater attachment, beat the butter with the chestnut paste. Using a whisk, beat the yolks with ⅓ cup (60 g) of the superfine sugar until thick and pale. Beat the egg whites until stiff with the remaining sugar. Combine the three mixtures, sift the flour with the starch, and incorporate the wet ingredients into the dry. On a baking sheet lined with a Silpat mat, spread a thin layer of the batter and sprinkle with candied chestnut pieces. Bake for 13 minutes.

FOR ASSEMBLY

Whip the ganache with a hand mixer. Pipe ganache over the entire surface of a 7-inch (18-cm)-diameter Pavoni silicone entremets mold. Pipe more in the middle so the insert will be well centered. Cut out a 7-inch (18-cm)-diameter disk from the chestnut sponge and insert it into the mold. Pipe a thin layer of ganache on top, then add a layer of chestnut cream and insert the meringue disk. Fill to the top with ganache and smooth with a spatula (palette knife). Freeze for about 4 hours until set.

FOR FINISHING

Use a pastry (piping) bag fitted with a size 236 vermicelli tip (nozzle) to pipe chestnut cream vermicelli in large semicircles, starting at the bottom of the cake and gradually working your way to the top. Start each semicircle in the middle of the preceding one. Refrigerate for about 4 hours before serving.

CHOUX TARDROPS

For the choux pastry

❋

⅓ cup plus 1½ tablespoons (100 g)
milk

⅝ teaspoon (4 g) salt

2 teaspoons (8 g) superfine
(caster) sugar

6½ tablespoons (90 g) unsalted
butter

¾ cup plus 1 tablespoon (110 g)
bread (strong) flour

3¼ extra-large (UK large/180 g)
eggs (⅔ cup)

Pearl sugar

For the vanilla Chantilly cream

❋

See page 335

FOR THE CHOUX PASTRY

In a saucepan, combine ⅓ cup plus 1 tablespoon (100 g) water with the
milk, salt, superfine sugar, and butter and bring to a boil. Let boil for
1-2 minutes, then add the flour and stir over low heat until the paste pulls
away easily from the sides of the pan. Transfer to a stand mixer fitted
with a flat beater attachment. Mix to release the steam, then add the eggs
in three batches. Refrigerate for about 2 hours. On a baking sheet lined
with a Silpain perforated baking mat, pipe lines of choux pastry, gradually
releasing the pressure from your hand to create teardrop shapes. Sprinkle
with the pearl sugar. Bake in a deck oven at 350°F (175°C) for 30 minutes
(or in a conventional oven, preheated to 500°F/260°C/Gas Mark 10, introduce
the baking sheet and turn off the oven for 15 minutes, then turn it back on
and continue baking at 325°F/160°C/Gas Mark 3 for 10 minutes).

FOR THE VANILLA CHANTILLY CREAM

Make the vanilla Chantilly cream as described on page 335.

FOR ASSEMBLY

Whip the Chantilly cream with a hand mixer. Cut the choux pastry teardrops
in half lengthwise across the middle. Use a pastry (piping) bag fitted with
a star tip (nozzle) to pipe Chantilly cream over the bottom halves. Cover
with the top halves.

OPERA

For the coffee ganache

See page 338

For the coffee sponge cake

½ cup plus ½ tablespoon (1 stick plus ½ tablespoons/120 g) unsalted butter, melted

¾ cup (140 g) coffee paste

6½ extra-large (UK large/240 g) egg whites (1 cup)

1 cup (180 g) superfine (caster) sugar

8½ extra-large (UK large/160 g) egg yolks (⅓ cup)

2 tablespoons (15 g) all-purpose (plain) flour

1½ tablespoons (15 g) potato starch

For the ristretto gel

2 cups (500 g) ristretto (concentrated espresso) coffee

2 tablespoons (25 g) superfine (caster) sugar

2⅝ teaspoons (7 g) agar powder

For the coffee crisp

See page 337

For the coffee crémeux

See page 336

For the opera glaze

13¼ ounces (375 g) brown compound coating

4⅜ ounces (125 g) semisweet (dark) chocolate

¼ cup plus 1½ teaspoons (65 g) grapeseed oil

For assembly

Unsweetened cocoa powder

1¾ ounces (50 g) semisweet (dark) chocolate

1 pinch charcoal black food coloring

FOR THE COFFEE GANACHE

Make the coffee ganache as described on page 338.

FOR THE COFFEE SPONGE CAKE

Preheat the oven to 410°F (210°C/Gas Mark 6). Mix the melted butter with the coffee paste. Beat the egg whites, gradually adding ½ cup plus 1½ tablespoons (120 g) of the sugar until stiff. Beat the yolks with the remaining sugar. Mix the white and yolk mixtures, then incorporate the butter and coffee mixture, flour, and starch. On a baking sheet lined with a Silpat mat, spread a thin layer of batter and bake for 4 minutes. Use a pastry cutter to cut out a 7-inch (18-cm)-diameter flower.

FOR THE RISTRETTO GEL

In a saucepan, bring the ristretto coffee to a boil, then add the sugar and agar powder. Incorporate using an immersion (stick) blender and refrigerate until set. Blend again.

FOR THE COFFEE CRISP

Make the coffee crisp as described on page 337.

FOR THE COFFEE CRÉMEUX

Make the coffee crémeux as described on page 336.

FOR THE OPERA GLAZE

In a saucepan, melt the compound coating at 104°F (40°C) with the chocolate, then add the oil.

FOR ASSEMBLY

Whip the ganache with a hand mixer. Spread a thin layer of crisp in a 7-inch (18-cm) diameter flower-shape mold. Place the sponge flower on top. Cover with a thin layer of crémeux, then with a layer of ristretto gel. Finish with a layer of ganache. On a rack, cover the cake with the melted glaze. Dust with the cocoa powder. Melt the chocolate and add the charcoal black coloring. Use a paper cone (or a pastry/piping bag fitted with a size 1 plain tip/nozzle) to pipe the word "Opera" in the middle.

CHRISTMAS BONNET

For the vanilla and kirsch ganache

◆

2⅔ cups (625 g) whipping cream

1 vanilla bean (pod), split
and scraped

5 ounces (140 g) white couverture
chocolate, chopped

2 tablespoons (35 g) gelatin mass
(1½ teaspoons/5 g gelatin powder
hydrated in 2 tablespoons/30 g
water)

½ cup (125 g) kirsch

**For the chocolate and fleur de sel
shortbread**

◆

See page 343

For the chocolate sponge cake

◆

1 cup (100 g) ground almonds

⅓ cup plus 1 tablespoon (90 g)
packed brown sugar

⅓ cup (40 g) all-purpose (plain)
flour

(4 g) baking powder

10 g) unsweetened cocoa powder

5 g salt

4 large (UK medium/135 g) egg
whites

2⅓ large (UK medium/40 g) egg
yolks (2½ tablespoons)

1½ tablespoons (25 g) whipping
cream

3 tablespoons (40 g) unsalted
butter, melted

1½ tablespoons (20 g) superfine
(caster) sugar

For the vanilla crémeux

◆

See page 336

For the morello cherry insert

◆

2 cups (500 g) morello cherry puree

2¼ teaspoons (6 g) xanthan gum

3¾ cups (750 g) candied morello
cherries

½ cup (125 g) morello cherries in
syrup

For the ruby chocolate coating

◆

See page 338

For the white chocolate coating

◆

See page 338

FOR THE VANILLA AND KIRSCH GANACHE

The previous day, heat half the cream in a saucepan. Add the split and scraped vanilla bean and seeds. Remove from the heat, cover, and let infuse for about 10 minutes. Heat the mixture again and filter through a conical sieve. Pour it over the chopped chocolate and gelatin mass. Incorporate the kirsch and cream using an immersion (stick) blender until the ganache is smooth. Refrigerate for about 12 hours.

FOR THE CHOCOLATE AND FLEUR DE SEL SHORTBREAD

Make the chocolate and fleur de sel shortbread as described on page 343. Let cool and cut out a 5-inch (13-cm)-diameter disk with a pastry cutter.

FOR THE CHOCOLATE SPONGE CAKE

Preheat the oven to 350°F (175°C/Gas Mark 4). Mix the ground almonds, brown sugar, flour, baking powder, cocoa powder, and salt with 1½ tablespoons (25 g) of the egg whites, the egg yolks, and cream. Add the melted butter. Beat the remaining egg whites, then add the superfine sugar and beat until stiff. Fold the beaten egg whites into the batter. Put a 4-inch (10-cm)-diameter pastry ring onto a baking sheet lined with a Silpat mat and pipe in the batter. Bake for 8 minutes, turning the tray halfway through.

FOR THE MORELLO CHERRY INSERT MIXTURE

Combine the puree with the xanthan gum and incorporate using an immersion (stick) blender, then add the cherries.

FOR THE VANILLA CRÉMEUX

Make the vanilla crémeux as described on page 336. Use it to make a 2⅛-inch (5.5-cm) sphere in a silicone mold and freeze it for 4 hours.

FOR THE RUBY AND WHITE CHOCOLATE COATINGS

Make the ruby chocolate coating, followed by the white coating, as described on page 338.

BONNET ASSEMBLY

Whip the ganache with a hand mixer. Pipe ganache over the entire inside surface of a 5½-inch (14-cm)-diameter silicone hemispherical mold. Cover with a layer of morello cherry insert mixture and top with the sponge disk. Add a thin layer of ganache to create a smooth surface. Lay the shortbread disk on top. Add more ganache and smooth with a spatula (palette knife). Freeze for about 4 hours.

FOR FiNiSHiNG

Step 1
Make the bonnet. Carefully unmold the hemisphere. Use a pastry (piping) bag fitted with a size 20 Saint-Honoré tip (nozzle) to pipe thick lines of ganache. Start at the center of the cake and pipe downward. Use a spray gun to uniformly flock the bonnet with ruby chocolate coating before serving.

Step 2
Make the pompon (pom-pom). Use a pastry bag fitted with a size 20 Saint-Honoré tip to pipe small flames of ganache over the frozen vanilla crémeux sphere. Use a spray gun to uniformly flock the pompon with white chocolate coating. Place it on the bonnet. Refrigerate for about 4 hours before serving.

MILK CHOCOLATE

For the milk chocolate ganache

2 ⅔ cups (625 g) whipping cream

1 vanilla bean (pod)

5 ounces (140 g) Alain Ducasse milk chocolate, chopped

2 tablespoons (35 g) gelatin mass (1½ teaspoons/5 g gelatin powder hydrated in 2 tablespoons/30 g water)

For the vanilla crémeux

See page 336

For the milk chocolate and vanilla crisp

2 vanilla beans (pods), split and scraped

1 ⅓ cups (200 g) almonds

⅓ cup (70 g) superfine (caster) sugar

3 ⅔ cups (200 g) feuilletine flakes

1½ tablespoons (20 g) grapeseed oil

3½ ounces (100 g) Alain Ducasse milk chocolate, melted

For the milk chocolate caramel sauce

¼ cup (50 g) superfine (caster) sugar

⅓ cup (80 g) glucose powder

½ cup (130 g) milk

½ cup plus 1 tablespoon (135 g) whipping cream

½ teaspoon (2 g) fleur de sel

3 tablespoons (40 g) unsalted butter

1¾ ounces (50 g) Alain Ducasse milk chocolate, chopped

For the milk chocolate coating

See page 338

FOR THE MiLK CHOCOLATE GANACHE

The previous day, heat half the cream in a saucepan. Add the split and scraped vanilla bean and seeds. Remove from the heat, cover, and let infuse for about 10 minutes. Heat the mixture again and filter through a conical sieve. Pour it over the chopped chocolate, gelatin mass, and the remaining cream. Incorporate using an immersion (stick) blender until the ganache is smooth. Refrigerate for about 12 hours.

FOR THE VANiLLA CRÉMEUX

Make the vanilla crémeux as described on page 336.

FOR THE MiLK CHOCOLATE AND VANiLLA CRiSP

Roast the vanilla beans and almonds in the oven at 325°F (165°C/Gas Mark 3) for 15 minutes. Make a dry caramel with the sugar; this should yield 1½ tablespoons (30 g). Pour the hot caramel over the vanilla beans. Let cool until solid. Use an immersion blender to process, separately, the feuilletine flakes, followed by the caramel and vanilla, then the almonds while gradually incorporating the oil. In a stand mixer fitted with a flat beater attachment, mix all the ingredients together while gradually adding the melted milk chocolate. Pipe a thin layer of crisp inside an 8-inch (20-cm) square pastry ring. Freeze for about 30 minutes.

FOR THE MiLK CHOCOLATE CARAMEL SAUCE

In a saucepan, heat the sugar and ¼ cup (55 g) of the glucose to 365°F (185°C) and cook to an amber caramel. In another saucepan, heat 3½ tablespoons (50 g) of the milk and the cream with the remaining glucose and the fleur de sel. Deglaze the caramel with the hot milk mixture. Cook until the temperature reaches 220°F (105°C), then filter through a conical sieve. When the temperature of the caramel drops to 170°F (70°C), add the butter, chopped chocolate, and remaining milk. Incorporate using an immersion blender and filter through a conical sieve.

FOR THE MiLK CHOCOLATE COATiNG

Make the milk chocolate coating as described on page 338.

FOR ASSEMBLY

Whip the ganache with a hand mixer. Following an arabesque pattern, line the entire interior surface of an 8-inch (20-cm) square mold, including the sides, with a thin layer of ganache. Spread over the top with a layer of vanilla crémeux, then with a layer of caramel sauce. Insert the crisp square and fill to the top with ganache. Smooth with a spatula (palette knife). Freeze for about 3 hours. Carefully unmold, then use a spray gun to uniformly flock the entremets with milk chocolate coating. Refrigerate for about 4 hours before serving.

BLOOD ORANGE

For the verbena pepper ganache

2¼ cups (530 g) whipping cream

½ cup (120 g) milk

1½ teaspoons (3 g) verbena peppercorns

5⅛ ounces (145 g) white chocolate, chopped

1½ tablespoons (25 g) gelatin mass (1 teaspoon/3.5 g) gelatin powder hydrated in 1½ tablespoons/21.5 g water)

For the joconde cake

See page 335

For the blood orange gel

⅓ cup plus 2 tablespoons (100 g) blood orange juice

2½ teaspoons (10 g) superfine (caster) sugar

¾ teaspoon (2 g) agar powder

For the lemon gel

⅓ cup plus 1 tablespoon (100 g) lemon juice

2½ teaspoons (10 g) superfine (caster) sugar

¾ teaspoon (2 g) agar powder

For the blood orange marmalade

⅔ cup (150 g) orange juice

(15 g) superfine (caster) sugar

3¾ teaspoons (2.5 g) agar powder

⅜ teaspoon (1 g) xanthan gum

⅓ cup plus 1½ tablespoons (75 g) candied blood orange peel

¼ cup (25 g) blood orange zest

½ cup (75 g) blood orange pulp

⅝ teaspoon (1 g) ground verbena pepper

½ teaspoon (1 g) verbena peppercorns

For the ruby chocolate coating

See page 338

FOR THE VERBENA PEPPER GANACHE

The previous day, heat half the cream in a saucepan with the verbena peppercorns. Pour it over the chopped chocolate and gelatin mass. Incorporate using an immersion (stick) blender, adding the remaining cream, until the ganache is smooth. Filter through a conical sieve and refrigerate for about 12 hours.

FOR THE JOCONDE CAKE

Make the joconde cake as described on page 335. Let cool, then cut out a 6¼-inch (16-cm)-diameter disk.

FOR THE BLOOD ORANGE GEL

In a saucepan, bring the juice to a boil. Mix together the sugar and agar powder. Incorporate using an immersion blender and refrigerate for about 2 hours, until set. Blend again before use.

FOR THE LEMON GEL

In a saucepan, bring the juice to a boil. Mix together the sugar and agar powder. Incorporate using an immersion blender and refrigerate for about 2 hours, until set. Blend again before use.

FOR THE BLOOD ORANGE MARMALADE

In a saucepan, bring the juice to a boil, then add the sugar mixed with the agar powder. Let cool, then add the xanthan gum and mix with an immersion blender. Incorporate the candied blood orange peel and blood orange zest and pulp, cut into cubes, along with the verbena pepper.

FOR THE INSERT

Lay the joconde disk inside a 6¼-inch (16-cm)-diameter and 1¼-inch (3-cm)-deep pastry ring. Pipe a layer of marmalade over the top. Add dots of lemon and blood orange gel. Freeze for about 3 hours.

FOR THE RUBY CHOCOLATE COATING

Make the ruby chocolate coating as described on page 338.

FOR ASSEMBLY

Whip the ganache with a hand mixer. Pipe ganache over the bottom and sides of an 8-inch (20-cm)-diameter rose-shape Pavoni mold. Pipe more in the middle so the insert will be well centered. Place the insert in the center. Fill to the top with ganache and smooth with a spatula (palette knife). Freeze for about 6 hours. Carefully unmold, then use a spray gun to uniformly flock the entremets with the coating.

TRUFFLE

For the chocolate ganache

2 1/3 cups (550 g) whipping cream

1¾ ounces (50 g) (bittersweet) dark chocolate (66% cocoa), chopped

3¾ teaspoons (21 g) gelatin mass (1 teaspoon/3 g gelatin powder hydrated in 3¾ teaspoons/18 g water)

For the chocolate tart shell

See page 342

For the praline and cocoa nib crisp

¾ cup (100 g) hazelnuts

2½ tablespoons (30 g) superfine (caster) sugar

1/3 cup (40 g) cocoa nibs

3 tablespoons (40 g) grapeseed oil

½ teaspoon (2 g) fleur de sel

1 cup (50 g) feuilletine flakes

For the truffle cream

⅞ cup (200 g) whipping cream

⅛ ounce (5 g) black truffle pieces

1 pinch fleur de sel

1½ teaspoons (4 g) xanthan gum

1 teaspoon (5 g) truffle oil

For assembly

Truffle pieces

Cocoa nibs

1 black truffle

FOR THE CHOCOLATE GANACHE

The previous day, heat half the cream in a saucepan. Pour it over the chopped chocolate and gelatin mass. Incorporate using an immersion (stick) blender, gradually adding the remaining cream, until the ganache is smooth. Filter through a conical sieve and refrigerate for about 12 hours.

FOR THE CHOCOLATE TART SHELL

Make the chocolate tart shell (case) as described on page 342.

FOR THE PRALINE AND COCOA NIB CRISP

Roast the hazelnuts in the oven for 15 minutes. Make a dry caramel with the sugar. Let cool, then process in a food processor until it forms a paste. Blend the hazelnuts with the cocoa nibs and oil. In a stand mixer fitted with a flat beater, mix all the ingredients together and add the feuilletine flakes.

FOR THE TRUFFLE CREAM

In a saucepan, combine the cream with the truffle pieces and salt and bring to a boil. Incorporate using an immersion blender, filter through a conical sieve, and let cool. Blend in the xanthan gum and truffle oil.

FOR ASSEMBLY

Pipe a layer of praline and cocoa nib crisp inside the tart shell. Add a layer of lightly whipped ganache. Sprinkle with truffle pieces, then cover with a thin layer of truffle cream. Fill the tart shell to the top with cocoa nibs. Use a truffle shaver (or a mandoline) to cut thin slices of truffle and arrange them in a rosette pattern over the tart.

TREE  iN

B⬤⬤OM

BASIC COMPONENTS

⬤ For the white chocolate ganache
4¼ cup (1 kg) whipping cream
5½ pounds (2.25 kg) white
chocolate, chopped

CRISPS

ALMOND AND HONEY

⬤ For the almond and honey praline
See page 342
⬤ For the almond and honey crisp
1 quantity (2¼ pounds/1 kg) almond
and honey praline
⅓ cup (50 g) pollen
5½ cups (300 g) feuilletine flakes
⅓ cup (75 g) cocoa butter

PECAN

⬤ For the pecan praline
See page 343
⬤ For the pecan crisp
See page 337

PISTACHIO

⬤ For the pistachio praline
See page 343
⬤ For the pistachio crisp
See page 337

ALMOND AND TIMUT PEPPER

⬤ For the almond and timut pepper
crisp
See page 337

COCONUT

⬤ For the coconut praline
See page 342
⬤ For the coconut crisp
See page 337

VANILLA

⬤ For the vanilla crisp
See page 337

HAZELNUT

⬤ For the hazelnut crisp
See page 337

The basic idea for creating the tree in bloom is to make spheres in the desired flavor of crisp and decorate them as different types of flowers by piping over them with white chocolate ganache using the techniques presented in this book. You can flock the flowers as desired (see the recipes for colored chocolate coatings given on page 338 of the Basic Recipes section), giving free rein to your creativity. The flowers must be well frozen for the assembly process. They are attached to a trunk made of white chocolate.

FOR THE WHITE CHOCOLATE GANACHE

Bring the cream to a boil, then pour it over the chopped chocolate and stir to combine.

FOR THE ALMOND AND HONEY

Make the almond and honey praline as described on page 342.

For the almond and honey crisp, melt the cocoa butter and mix with the remaining ingredients.

PECAN

Make the pecan praline as described on page 343 and the pecan crisp as described on page 337.

PISTACHIO

Make the pistachio praline as described on page 343 and the pistachio crisp as described on page 337.

ALMOND AND TIMUT PEPPER

Make the almond and timut pepper crisp as described on page 337.

COCONUT

Make the coconut praline as described on page 342 and the coconut crisp as described on page 337.

VANILLA

Make the vanilla crisp as described on page 337.

HAZELNUT

Make the hazelnut crisp as described on page 337.

Pipe each crisp mixture into ¾-, 1¼-, or 1½-inch (2-, 3-, or 4-cm)-diameter spherical silicone molds. Freeze for about 2 hours until set. Carefully unmold, then use a size 104 Saint-Honoré tip (nozzle) or a plain tip to decorate with the ganache. Flock some of the flowers to create an appealing visual effect.

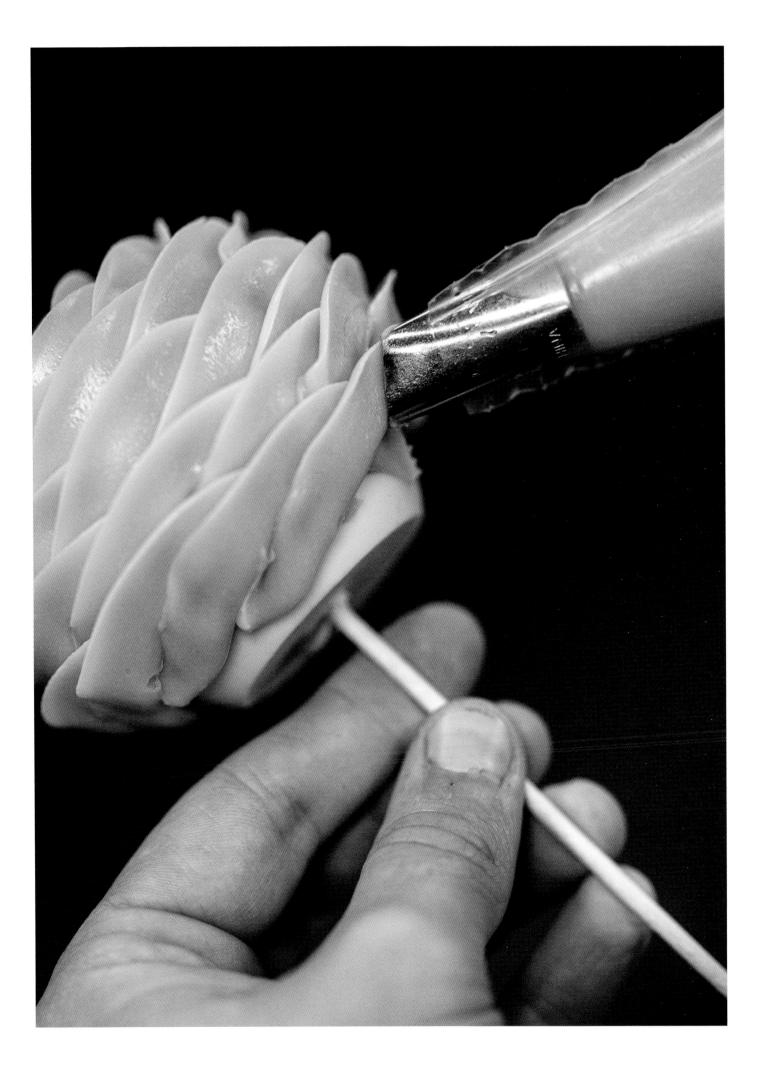

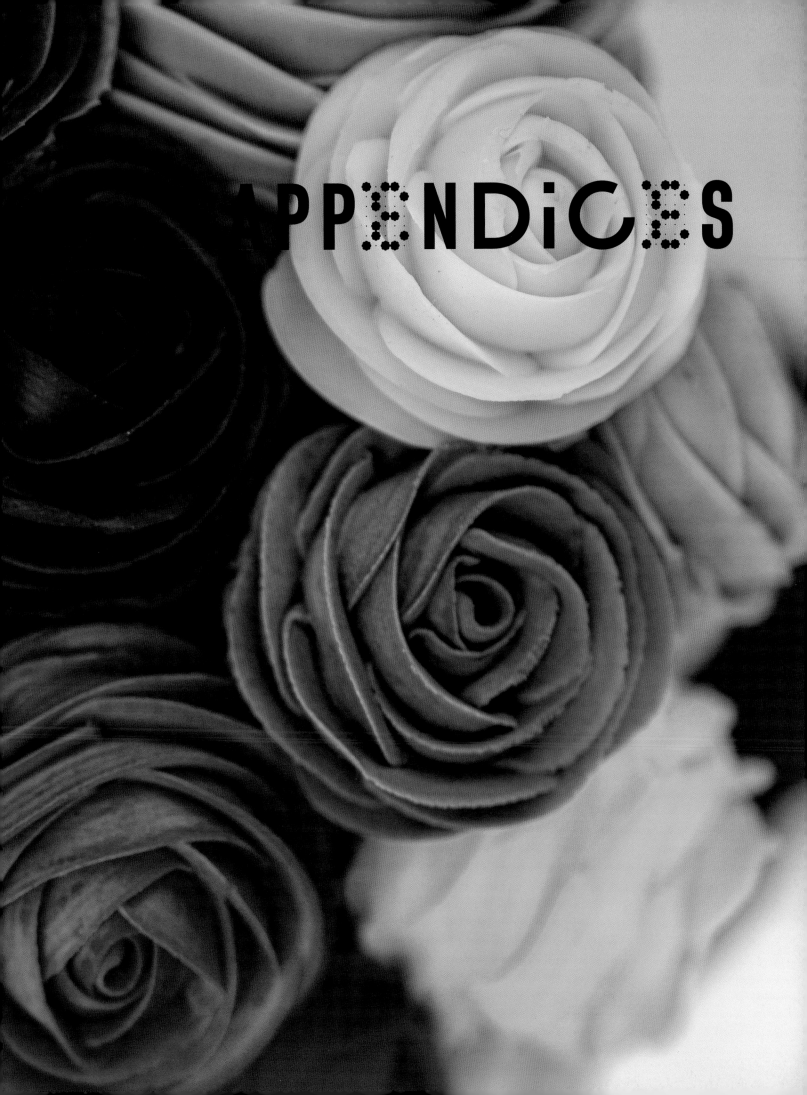

APPENDICES

BASIC RECIPES

JOCONDE CAKE

● 3 large (UK medium/140 g) eggs

⅞ cup (105 g) confectioners'
(icing) sugar

1⅛ cups (105 g) ground almonds

¼ cup (30 g) all-purpose (plain)
flour

1½ tablespoons (20 g) unsalted
butter, melted

4¼ large (UK medium/90 g) egg
whites (⅜ cup)

3¾ teaspoons (15 g) superfine
(caster) sugar

Preheat the oven to 350°F (175°C/Gas Mark 4). In a stand mixer fitted with a whisk attachment, beat the eggs with the confectioners' sugar and ground almonds. Incorporate the flour and melted butter. Beat the egg whites until stiff with the superfine sugar. Fold the beaten egg whites into the batter. Spread the batter over a baking sheet lined with a Silpat mat. Bake for 10 minutes.

PAIN DE GÊNES CAKE

● 5 tablespoons (70 g) unsalted
butter

1¼ cups (120 g) ground almonds

3 large (UK medium/150 g) eggs

2 tablespoons (20 g) bread (strong)
flour, sifted

2 tablespoons (20 g) potato starch

1 cup (120 g) confectioners'
(icing) sugar

Preheat the oven to 350°F (175°C/Gas Mark 4). In a saucepan, heat the butter to 115°F (45°C). Mix the ground almonds with the eggs, then transfer to a stand mixer and beat until smooth. Incorporate the sifted flour, starch, and sugar, followed by the melted butter. Spread the batter inside a 7-inch (18-cm)-diameter pastry ring and bake for about 20 minutes. Let cool.

FLAKY BRIOCHE

● ⅓ cup plus 1½ tablespoons
(100 g) milk

¾ small cake (13 g) fresh yeast, or
2¼ teaspoons active dry (easy-blend)
yeast, dissolved in milk or water

2 cups (285 g) bread (strong) flour

⅝ teaspoon (4 g) salt

1½ tablespoons (20 g) superfine
(caster) sugar

1 large (UK medium/50 g) egg

1¾ tablespoons (25 g) unsalted
butter, softened

⅝ cup (150 g) unsalted dry butter
(84% fat content)

Preheat the oven to 350°F (175°C/Gas Mark 4). In a stand mixer fitted with a dough hook, combine the milk, yeast, flour, salt, and sugar and mix on speed 1 while gradually adding the eggs. Increase to speed 2 and continue mixing until the dough pulls away from the sides. Cut the softened butter into cubes, incorporate it into the dough, and knead until smooth. Let the dough rise at room temperature (68-77°F/20-25°C) for about 1 hour. Use your palms to flatten and deflate the dough, then roll out into a rectangle. Shape the dry butter into a rectangle half the size and place it in the center of the dough. Fold over the sides of the dough to encase the butter and roll out, then fold with a simple turn (letter fold). Roll out the dough again, then fold with a double turn (book fold). Roll it out again and finish by folding with a simple turn. Refrigerate. Roll out the dough and use it to line a 6-inch (15-cm)-diameter flower-shape baking pan previously lined with parchment (baking) paper. Cover with another layer of parchment paper. Fill with pie weights (baking beans) to ensure the tart shell retains the shape of the pan. Bake for 15 minutes.

CARAMEL SAUCE

● ¼ cup (50 g) superfine (caster)
sugar

⅓ cup (80 g) glucose powder

1½ tablespoons (25 g) milk

⅓ cup 2 tablespoons (105 g)
whipping cream

1 teaspoon (2 g) vanilla pearls
(or vanilla seeds)

¼ teaspoon (1 g) fleur de sel

3 tablespoons (40 g) unsalted butter

In a saucepan, heat the sugar and ¼ cup (55 g) of the glucose to 365°F (185°C) and cook to an amber caramel. In another saucepan, heat the milk and cream with the remaining glucose, the vanilla pearls, and fleur de sel. Deglaze the caramel with this mixture. Cook until the temperature reaches 220°F (105°C), then filter through a conical sieve. When the temperature of the caramel drops to 160°F (70°C), incorporate the butter using an immersion (stick) blender.

VANILLA CHANTILLY CREAM

● 1¾ cups (430 g) whipping cream

2 vanilla beans (pods), split and
scraped

3¾ teaspoons (15 g) superfine
(caster) sugar

3 tablespoons (45 g) mascarpone cheese

2½ tablespoons (14 g) gelatin mass
(⅝ teaspoon/2 g gelatin powder hydrated
in 2½ tablespoons/12 g water)

In a saucepan, combine one-third of the cream with the vanilla beans and seeds and the sugar, then bring to a boil. Pour the boiling mixture over the mascarpone and gelatin mass. Filter through a conical sieve and incorporate using an immersion (stick) blender, gradually adding the remaining cream. Refrigerate.

ALMOND CREAM

- 4½ tablespoons (65 g) unsalted butter, softened
- 1/3 cup (65 g) superfine (caster) sugar
- 2/3 cup (65 g) ground almonds
- 2 small (65 g) eggs

In a stand mixer fitted with a flat beater attachment, cream the butter with the sugar and ground almonds. Gradually incorporate the eggs, then refrigerate.

ALMOND AND VANiLLA CREAM

- 4½ tablespoons (65 g) unsalted butter, softened
- 1/3 cup (65 g) superfine (caster) sugar
- 2/3 cup (65 g) ground almonds
- ¼ cup (25 g) vanilla pearls (or vanilla seeds)
- 2 small (65 g) eggs

In a stand mixer fitted with a flat beater attachment, cream the butter with the sugar, ground almonds, and vanilla pearls. Gradually incorporate the eggs, then refrigerate.

CRÈME DiPLOMAT

- 2 tablespoons (35 g) gelatin mass (1½ teaspoons/5 g gelatin powder hydrated in 2 tablespoons/30g water)
- 1⅓ cups (265 g) vanilla ganache (recipe on page 340)
- 1 cup (265 g) vanilla pastry cream (recipe below)

Melt the gelatin mass. In a large bowl, mix it with the pastry cream. Whip the ganache with a hand mixer. Incorporate in three batches into the vanilla pastry cream mixture.

VANiLLA PASTRY CREAM

- ½ cup plus 1 tablespoon (140 g) milk
- 1½ tablespoons (25 g) whipping cream
- 1 vanilla bean (pod)
- 3 medium (UK small/45 g) egg yolks
- 3½ tablespoons (40 g) superfine (caster) sugar
- 2 teaspoons (12 g) custard powder
- 1 tablespoon (15 g) unsalted butter, softened
- 2 tablespoons (30 g) mascarpone cheese

In a saucepan, combine the milk with the cream and bring to a boil. Add the split and scraped vanilla bean and seeds, then remove from the heat. Cover and let infuse for about 10 minutes. Bring back to a boil and filter through a conical sieve. In the meantime, using a whisk, beat the yolks in a large bowl with the sugar and custard powder until thick and pale. Add the boiling mixture. Let boil for 2 minutes before incorporating the butter and mascarpone.

COFFEE CRÈMEUX

- 2 cups (500 g) milk
- 5¼ large (UK medium/90 g) egg yolks (⅜ cup)
- 3 tablespoons (35 g) superfine (caster) sugar
- 1/3 cup (75 g) coffee paste
- 1 teaspoon (2.5 g) xanthan gum

In a saucepan, heat the milk to just before boiling. Using a whisk, beat the egg yolks with the sugar and coffee paste until thick and pale. Pour this mixture into the milk and cook for 1-2 minutes. Let cool, then incorporate the xanthan gum using an immersion (stick) blender. Filter through a conical sieve and refrigerate.

VANiLLA CRÈMEUX

- 2 cups (500 g) milk
- 3 vanilla beans (pods)
- 5¼ large (UK medium/90 g) egg yolks (⅜ cup)
- 3 tablespoons (35 g) superfine (caster) sugar

In a saucepan, combine the milk with the vanilla beans and seeds, then bring to a boil. Using a whisk, beat the egg yolks with the sugar until thick and pale. Add part of the hot milk. Add the mixture to the remaining milk in the pan and heat to 180°F (83°C). Filter through a conical sieve, blend, and let cool.

ALMOND AND HONEY CRiSP

- 1/3 cup (75 g) cocoa butter
- 1 quantity (1 kg) almond and honey praline (see recipe page 342)
- 1/3 cup (50 g) pollen
- 5½ cups (300 g) feuilletine flakes

In a saucepan, melt the cocoa butter and mix in the remaining ingredients.

ALMOND AND TIMUT PEPPER CRISP

- 3½ cups (500 g) unblanched almonds
- ⅔ cup (130 g) superfine (caster) sugar
- ¼ cup (50 g) cocoa butter, melted
- 1⅞ cups (100 g) feuilletine flakes
- 4¾ teaspoons (10 g) timut peppercorns
- ½ teaspoon (2 g) fleur de sel

Dry the almonds in the oven at 210°F (100°C) for 1 hour. In a saucepan, combine 2½ tablespoons (40 g) water with the sugar and heat to 230°F (110°C). Add the dried almonds and coat well with the syrup. Let cool, then use an immersion (stick) blender to crush and blend the almonds with the melted cocoa butter, feuilletine flakes, timut peppercorns, and fleur de sel.

COFFEE CRISP

- 1⅞ cups (250 g) hazelnuts
- ⅓ cup (75 g) superfine (caster) sugar
- 1¼ teaspoons (5 g) fleur de sel
- ⅓ cup (75 g) coffee paste, strained
- 2 tablespoons (25 g) cocoa butter, melted
- 1⅞ cups (100 g) feuilletine flakes

Roast the hazelnuts in the oven at 325°F (165°C/Gas Mark 3) for 15 minutes. Make a dry caramel with the sugar. Let cool, then process using an immersion (stick) blender. Crush and blend the hazelnuts with the fleur de sel and coffee paste. Incorporate the melted cocoa butter, followed by the feuilletine flakes.

COCONUT CRISP

- 1 quantity (500 g) coconut praline (see recipe on page 342)
- 2¾ cups (150 g) feuilletine flakes
- 3 tablespoons (40 g) cocoa butter, melted

Mix the praline with the feuilletine flakes and melted cocoa butter.

HAZELNUT CRISP

- ¾ cup (100 g) hazelnuts
- 3 tablespoons (35 g) superfine (caster) sugar
- 1⅞ cups (100 g) feuilletine flakes
- 2½ teaspoons (10 g) grapeseed oil
- 2¼ teaspoons (10 g) cocoa butter, melted

Roast the hazelnuts in the oven at 325°F (165°C/Gas Mark 3) for 15 minutes. Make a dry caramel with the sugar; it should yield 1½ tablespoons (30 g). Let cool until solid. Use an immersion (stick) blender to process, separately, the feuilletine flakes, followed by the caramel, then the hazelnuts while gradually incorporating the oil. In a stand mixer fitted with a flat beater attachment, mix all the ingredients together while gradually adding the melted cocoa butter.

PECAN CRISP

- 2½ cups (250 g) pecans
- ⅔ quantity (500 g) pecan praline (see recipe on page 343)
- 1⅞ cups (100 g) feuilletine flakes
- 2 tablespoons (25 g) cocoa butter, melted

Roast the pecans in the oven at 325°F (165°C/Gas Mark 3) for 15 minutes, then chop them. In a stand mixer fitted with a flat beater attachment, mix together the pecans, praline, and feuilletine flakes while gradually adding the melted cocoa butter.

PISTACHIO CRISP

- ⅔ quantity (650 g) pistachio praline (see recipe on page 343)
- 3½ cups (195 g) feuilletine flakes
- ¼ cup (50 g) cocoa butter, melted

In a stand mixer fitted with a flat beater attachment, mix together the praline and feuilletine flakes while gradually adding the melted cocoa butter. Spread a layer of the crisp inside a 6¼-inch (16-cm)-diameter pastry ring.

VANILLA CRISP

- 3 vanilla beans (pods)
- ⅔ cup (100 g) whole almonds
- 3 tablespoons (35 g) superfine (caster) sugar
- 2 cups (100 g) feuilletine flakes
- 2 teaspoons (10 g) grapeseed oil
- 2 teaspoons (10 g) cocoa butter, melted

Roast the vanilla beans and almonds in the oven at 325°F (165°C/Gas Mark 3) for 15 minutes. Make a dry caramel with the sugar; it should yield 1½ tablespoons (30 g). Pour the hot caramel over the vanilla beans. Let cool until solid. Use an immersion (stick) blender to process, separately, the feuilletine flakes, followed by the caramel and vanilla, then the almonds while gradually incorporating the oil. In a stand mixer fitted with a flat beater attachment, mix all the ingredients together while gradually adding the melted cocoa butter.

WHITE CHOCOLATE COATING

● ½ cup (100 g) cocoa butter
3½ ounces (100 g) white chocolate, chopped

In a saucepan, melt the cocoa butter, then pour it over the chopped chocolate. Incorporate using an immersion (stick) blender until smooth.

CHARCOAL BLACK CHOCOLATE COATING

● ½ cup (100 g) cocoa butter
3½ ounces (100 g) white chocolate, chopped
⅜ teaspoon (1 g) charcoal powder

In a saucepan, melt the cocoa butter, then pour it over the chopped chocolate. Incorporate the charcoal powder using an immersion (stick) blender until smooth.

MILK CHOCOLATE COATING

● ½ cup (100 g) cocoa butter
3½ ounces (100 g) milk chocolate, chopped

In a saucepan, melt the cocoa butter, then pour it over the chopped chocolate. Incorporate using an immersion (stick) blender until smooth.

YELLOW CHOCOLATE COATING

● ½ cup (100 g) cocoa butter
3½ ounces (100 g) white chocolate, chopped
scant ¼ teaspoon (1 g) yellow fat-soluble food coloring

In a saucepan, melt the cocoa butter, then pour it over the chopped chocolate. Add the food coloring and blend until smooth.

ORANGE CHOCOLATE COATING

● ½ cup (100 g) cocoa butter
3½ ounces (100 g) white chocolate, chopped
scant ¼ teaspoon (1 g) orange fat-soluble food coloring

In a saucepan, melt the cocoa butter, then pour it over the chopped chocolate. Add the food coloring and blend until smooth.

PINK CHOCOLATE COATING

● ½ cup (100 g) cocoa butter
3½ ounces (100 g) white chocolate, chopped
scant ⅛ teaspoon (0.5 g) red food coloring powder

In a saucepan, melt the cocoa butter, then pour it over the chopped chocolate. Add the food coloring and blend until smooth.

RUBY CHOCOLATE COATING

● ½ cup (100 g) cocoa butter
3½ ounces (100 g) white chocolate
scant ¼ teaspoon (1 g) red food coloring powder

In a saucepan, melt the cocoa butter, then pour it over the chopped chocolate. Add the food coloring and blend until smooth.

GREEN CHOCOLATE COATING

● ½ cup (100 g) cocoa butter
3½ ounces (100 g) white chocolate, chopped
scant ¼ teaspoon (1 g) green fat-soluble food coloring

In a saucepan, melt the cocoa butter, then pour it over the chopped chocolate. Add the food coloring and blend until smooth.

COFFEE GANACHE

● ⅞ cup (200 g) whipping cream
¼ cup (50 g) coffee beans
5 large (UK medium/85 g) egg yolks
3½ tablespoons (40 g) superfine (caster) sugar
1 tablespoon (17 g) gelatin mass (¾ teaspoon/2.5 g gelatin powder hydrated in 1 tablespoon/14.5 g water)
1½ cups (330 g) mascarpone cheese
⅓ cup (20 g) instant coffee powder

In a saucepan, combine the cream with the coffee beans and bring to a boil. Remove from the heat, cover, and let infuse for 10 minutes. Mix the yolks with the sugar. Bring the cream back to a boil and pour a little boiling cream over this mixture, then return it to the saucepan to make a crème anglaise. Cook for 2 minutes, filter through a conical sieve, and incorporate the gelatin mass using an immersion (stick) blender. Blend in the mascarpone and instant coffee powder and refrigerate for about 12 hours.

LEMON GANACHE

- 3⅓ cups (800 g) whipping cream
- 2½ tablespoons (42 g) gelatin mass (2 teaspoons/7 g gelatin powder hydrated in 2½ tablespoons/36 g water)
- 7½ ounces (215 g) ivory white couverture chocolate, chopped
- ¾ cup (180 g) lemon juice

The day before, heat half the cream in a saucepan, then add the gelatin mass. Gradually pour the mixture over the chopped chocolate. Whisk until smooth. Add the remaining cream, followed by the lemon juice. Incorporate using an immersion (stick) blender until smooth and refrigerate for about 12 hours.

LYCHEE AND VERBENA PEPPER GANACHE

- 2¼ cups (530 g) whipping cream
- 1½ teaspoons (3 g) verbena peppercorns
- 5⅛ ounces (145 g) white chocolate, chopped
- 5 teaspoons (28 g) gelatin mass (1¼ teaspoons/4 g gelatin powder hydrated in 5 teaspoons/24 g water)
- ⅓ cup plus 1½ tablespoons (100 g) lychee juice
- 4 teaspoons (20 g) lemon juice

The day before, combine half the cream with the peppercorns in a saucepan and bring to a boil. Remove from the heat, cover, and let infuse for about 5 minutes. Pour the hot cream over the chopped chocolate and gelatin mass. Incorporate using an immersion (stick) blender, adding the remaining cream, the lychee juice, and lemon juice. Filter through a conical sieve and refrigerate for about 12 hours.

PISTACHIO GANACHE

- 2 cups (500 g) whipping cream
- 3 large (UK medium/50 g) egg yolks
- 2 tablespoons (25 g) superfine (caster) sugar
- 1¾ teaspoons (10 g) gelatin mass (½ teaspoon/1.5 g gelatin powder hydrated in 1¾ teaspoons/8.5 g water)
- ⅔ cup (150 g) pistachio paste
- ⅞ cup (200 g) mascarpone cheese

In a saucepan, bring the cream to a boil. Beat the yolks with the sugar. Pour a little boiling cream over this mixture, then return it to the saucepan to make a crème anglaise. Cook for 2 minutes, then incorporate the gelatin mass and pistachio paste using an immersion (stick) blender. Filter through a conical sieve and add the mascarpone. Refrigerate for about 12 hours.

FOR THE TIMUT PEPPER GANACHE

- ⅞ cup (200 g) whipping cream
- 1⅛ teaspoons (2.5 g) timut peppercorns
- 5 large (UK medium/85 g) egg yolks
- 3½ tablespoons (40 g) superfine (caster) sugar
- 1 tablespoon (17 g) gelatin mass (¾ teaspoon/2.5 g gelatin powder hydrated in 1 tablespoon/14.5 g water)
- 1⅓ cups plus 1½ tablespoons (330 g) mascarpone cheese

In a saucepan, combine the cream with the peppercorns and bring to a boil. Beat the yolks with the sugar. Pour a little boiling cream over this mixture, then return it to the saucepan to make a crème anglaise. Cook for 2 minutes, then incorporate the gelatin mass using an immersion (stick) blender. Filter through a conical sieve and add the mascarpone. Refrigerate for about 12 hours.

VANILLA GANACHE

- 2 cups (470 g) whipping cream
- 1 vanilla bean (pod)
- 3½ ounces (100 g) ivory white couverture chocolate, chopped
- 5 teaspoons (28 g) gelatin mass (1¼ teaspoons/4 g gelatin powder hydrated in 5 teaspoons/24 g water)

The previous day, heat half the cream in a saucepan. Add the split and scraped vanilla bean and seeds. Remove from the heat, cover, and let infuse for about 10 minutes. Heat the mixture again and filter through a conical sieve. Pour it over the chopped chocolate and gelatin mass. Incorporate using an immersion (stick) blender, adding the remaining cream, until the ganache is smooth. Refrigerate for about 12 hours

STRAWBERRY GEL

- 1⅔ cups (400 g) strawberry juice
- 3½ tablespoons (40 g) superfine (caster) sugar
- 2¼ teaspoons (6 g) agar powder
- ¾ teaspoon (2 g) xanthan gum

In a saucepan, bring the strawberry juice to a boil, then add the sugar, agar, and xanthan gum. Incorporate using an immersion (stick) blender and refrigerate until set.

RASPBERRY GEL

● 1²/₃ cups (400 g) raspberry juice

3½ tablespoons (40 g) superfine (caster) sugar

2¼ teaspoons (6 g) agar powder

¾ teaspoon (2 g) xanthan gum

In a saucepan, bring the raspberry juice to a boil, then add the sugar, agar, and xanthan gum. Incorporate using an immersion (stick) blender and refrigerate until set.

PISTACHIO GEL

● 2 cups (500 g) pistachio milk

4¾ extra-large (UK large/90 g) egg yolks (⅜ cup)

3 tablespoons (35 g) superfine (caster) sugar

1 teaspoon (2.5 g) xanthan gum

⅓ cup (75 g) pistachio paste

In a saucepan, heat the pistachio milk to just before boiling. Using a whisk, beat the egg yolks with the sugar until thick and pale. Add part of the hot pistachio milk and let cook for 1-2 minutes. Let cool. Incorporate using an immersion (stick) blender, adding the xanthan gum and pistachio paste. Filter through a conical sieve and refrigerate.

PISTACHIO MILK

● 2 cups (500 g) milk

⅜ cup (50 g) pistachio nuts

Process the milk and pistachios in a juicer.

VANILLA GLAZE

● ⅓ cup (100 g) neutral glaze

½ teaspoon (1 g) vanilla pearls (or vanilla seeds)

In a saucepan, combine the neutral glaze with the vanilla pearls and bring to a boil.

MERINGUE

● 3¾ large (UK medium/125 g) egg whites (½ cup)

²/₃ cup (125 g) superfine (caster) sugar

1 cup (125 g) confectioners' (icing) sugar

Beat the egg whites until stiff, adding the superfine sugar in three batches. The meringue is ready when it forms a peak on the end of the whisk without collapsing. Fold in the confectioners' sugar, transfer to a pastry (piping) bag, and set aside.

BABA BATTER

● 1²/₃ cups (190 g) bread strong flour

⅜ teaspoon (2 g) salt

4 tablespoons (60 g) unsalted butter

⅜ small cake (7 g) fresh yeast, or 1¼ teaspoons active dry (easy-blend) yeast, dissolved in milk or water

1 teaspoon (7 g) golden (runny) honey

4¼ large UK medium/210 g) eggs (⅞ cup)

4 teaspoons (20 g) milk

In a stand mixer fitted with a dough hook, mix the flour, salt, butter, yeast, and honey. Add half of the eggs, then knead on speed 1. When the dough is smooth, scrape the bottom of the bowl, then gradually add the remaining eggs. Knead to give the dough a little body, then add the milk. Knead a little longer, then transfer the batter to a pastry (piping) bag.

CHOUX PUFFS

● 1¼ cups (300 g) milk

2 teaspoons (12 g) salt

2 tablespoons (25 g) superfine (caster) sugar

1 cup plus 3 tablespoons (2⅜ sticks/270 g) unsalted butter

2⅓ cups plus 1½ tablespoons (330 g) bread (strong) flour

10 large (UK medium/540 g) eggs

In a saucepan, combine 1¼ cups (300 g) water with the milk, salt, sugar, and butter and bring to a boil. Let boil for 1-2 minutes, then add the flour and stir over low heat until the paste pulls away easily from the sides of the pan. Transfer to a stand mixer fitted with a flat beater attachment. Mix to release the steam, then add the eggs in three batches. Refrigerate for about 2 hours. On a baking sheet lined with a Silpat mat (or parchment/baking paper), pipe ¾-inch (2-cm)-diameter choux puffs. Bake in a deck oven at 350°F (175°C) for 30 minutes (or in a conventional oven preheated to 500°F/260°C/Gas Mark 10; introduce the baking sheet and turn off the oven for 15 minutes, then turn it back on and continue baking at 325°F/160°C/Gas Mark 3 for 10 minutes).

DIAMOND SHORTBREAD TART SHELL

- ½ cup (1 stick/115 g) unsalted butter
- ½ cup plus 1 tablespoon (70 g) confectioners' (icing) sugar
- ¼ cup plus 2 teaspoons (25 g) ground hazelnuts
- scant ¼ teaspoon (1 g) salt
- 1 medium (UK small/45 g) egg
- 1⅜ cups (190 g) bread (strong) flour
- ⅜ cup (60 g) potato starch
- Egg white
- ½ cup (100 g) packed brown sugar
- 1½ tablespoons (20 g) packed muscovado sugar
- 4 teaspoons (20 g) coconut sugar

In a stand mixer fitted with a flat beater attachment, cream the butter with the confectioners' sugar, ground hazelnuts, and salt. Add and beat with the egg, then add the flour and starch. Mix until smooth. Refrigerate. Roll out the dough to an ⅛-inch (3-mm) thickness and cut out a 14-inch (35-cm)-diameter disk. Turn an 11-inch (28-cm)-diameter baking pan upside down and line the outside with the dough. Trim off the excess with a knife. Prick with a fork. Brush the entire surface of the dough lightly with egg white. Mix the brown, muscovado, and coconut sugars together and dust the dough, covering it completely. Place two Silpain perforated baking mats on top. Bake for 30 minutes.

SWEET TART SHELL

- ½ cup (1 stick/115 g) unsalted butter
- ½ cup plus 1 tablespoon (70 g) confectioners' (icing) sugar
- ¼ cup plus 2 teaspoons (25 g) ground hazelnuts
- scant ¼ teaspoon (1 g) salt
- 1 medium (UK small/45 g) egg
- 1⅜ cups (190 g) bread (strong) flour
- ⅜ cup (60 g) potato starch

Preheat the oven to 325°F (165°C/Gas Mark 3). In a stand mixer fitted with a flat beater attachment, cream the butter with the confectioners' sugar, ground hazelnuts, and salt. Add the egg and beat, then add the flour and starch. Mix until smooth. Refrigerate for 4 hours. Roll out the dough to an ⅛-inch (3-mm) thickness and cut out an 11¾-inch (30-cm)-diameter disk. Line an 8-inch (20-cm)-diameter pastry ring. Trim off the excess with a knife. Place the ring on a Silpat mat (or parchment/baking paper). Prick the tart shell (case) with a fork. Bake for 30 minutes.

CHOCOLATE TART SHELL

- ½ cup (1 stick/115 g) unsalted butter
- ½ cup plus 1 tablespoon (70 g) confectioners' (icing) sugar
- ¼ cup plus 2 teaspoons (25 g) ground hazelnuts
- scant ¼ teaspoon (1 g) salt
- 1 medium (UK small/45 g) egg
- 1⅜ cups (190 g) bread (strong) flour
- ⅜ cup (60 g) potato starch
- ½ cup plus 1 tablespoon (50 g) unsweetened cocoa powder

Preheat the oven to 325°F (165°C/Gas Mark 3). In a stand mixer fitted with a flat beater attachment, cream the butter with the confectioners' sugar, ground hazelnuts, and salt. Add and beat with the egg, then add the flour, starch, and cocoa powder. Mix until smooth. Refrigerate. Roll out the dough to an ⅛-inch (3-mm) thickness and cut out an 11¾-inch (30-cm)-diameter disk. Line a 8-inch (20-cm)-diameter pastry ring and trim off the excess with a knife. Place the ring on a Silpat mat (or parchment/baking paper). Prick the tart shell (case) with a fork and bake for 30 minutes.

ALMOND AND HONEY PRALINE

- 3¾ cups (500 g) whole almonds
- 1½ cups (500 g) lavender honey

Spread the almonds on a baking sheet and dry them in the oven at 210°F (100°C) for 1 hour 30 minutes. Heat the honey to 285°F (140°C) and add the dried almonds, coating them well in the syrup. Let cool, then process to a paste using an immersion (stick) blender.

COCONUT PRALINE

- ⅔ cup (100 g) whole almonds
- 4½ cups (325 g) shredded coconut
- 1 cup (180 g) superfine (caster) sugar
- ¾ teaspoon (3 g) fleur de sel

Roast the almonds and shredded coconut separately in the oven at 340°F (170°C/Gas Mark 3½) for 15 minutes. After taking the almonds out of the oven, wait 5 minutes, process to a paste using an immersion (stick) blender, then add the coconut. Make a dry caramel with the sugar. Let cool, then process to a paste. Mix with coconut and almond paste and the salt.

HAZELNUT PRALINE

- 2⅞ cups (380 g) hazelnuts
- ½ cup plus 1 tablespoon (115 g) superfine (caster) sugar
- 2 teaspoons (8 g) fleur de sel

Roast the hazelnuts in the oven at 325°F (165°C/Gas Mark 3) for 15 minutes. Make a dry caramel with the sugar. Let cool, then process to a paste. Grind the hazelnuts. In a stand mixer fitted with a flat beater, combine all the ingredients and mix thoroughly.

PECAN PRALINE

- 5 cups (500 g) pecans
- ⅔ cup (125 g) superfine (caster) sugar
- 2½ teaspoons (10 g) fleur de sel

Roast the pecans in the oven at 325°F (165°C/Gas Mark 3) for 15 minutes. Make a dry caramel with the sugar. Let cool, then process to a paste using an immersion blender. Grind the pecans. In a stand mixer fitted with a flat beater, combine all the ingredients and mix thoroughly.

PISTACHIO PRALINE

- 5⅞ cups (750 g) pistachio nuts
- 1⅛ cups (225 g) superfine (caster) sugar
- 3¾ teaspoons (15 g) fleur de sel

Roast the pistachios in the oven at 325°F (165°C/Gas Mark 3) for 15 minutes. Make a dry caramel with the sugar and let cool before processing to a paste. Grind the pistachios. In a stand mixer fitted with a flat beater, combine all the ingredients and mix thoroughly.

RECONSTITUTED BRETON SHORTBREAD

- 1 cup plus 1 tablespoon (2 sticks plus 1 tablespoon/240 g) unsalted butter
- ¼ cup (50 g) cocoa butter
- 1 cup plus 1 tablespoon (210 g) superfine (caster) sugar
- 5½ large (UK medium/95 g) egg yolks (⅜ cup)
- ⅞ teaspoon (5 g) salt
- 2⅞ cups (360 g) all-purpose (plain) flour
- 5⅝ teaspoons (25 g) baking powder

In a stand mixer fitted with a flat beater attachment, cream the butter with the cocoa butter and sugar. Add the yolks and salt. Incorporate the dry ingredients without giving the dough too much body. Roll out the dough to an ⅛-inch (3-mm) thickness and cut out an 8-inch (20-cm)-diameter disk. Place the disk on a baking sheet lined with a Silpat mat. Bake at 340°F (170°C/Gas Mark 3½) for about 20 minutes.

CHOCOLATE AND FLEUR DE SEL SHORTBREAD

- ¾ cup plus 1 tablespoon (1⅝ sticks/190 g) unsalted butter, softened
- ⅔ cup (150 g) packed brown sugar
- ⅓ cup (60 g) superfine (caster) sugar
- 1 teaspoon (2 g) vanilla pearls (or vanilla seeds)
- ¾ teaspoon (3 g) fleur de sel
- 1¾ cups (220 g) all-purpose (plain) flour
- ⅓ cup plus 1 tablespoon (35 g) unsweetened cocoa powder
- 6¾ ounces (190 g) bittersweet (dark) chocolate (70% cocoa)

Mix the butter with the brown sugar, superfine sugar, vanilla, and salt. Sift the flour and cocoa and incorporate. Add the chopped chocolate. Roll out the dough to an ⅛-inch (3-mm)-thickness, lay on a baking sheet lined with a Silpat mat, and bake at 340°F (170°C/Gas Mark 3½) for 9 minutes. Let cool, then finely chop.

BABA SOAKING SYRUP

- ⅔ cup (120 g) superfine (caster) sugar
- 1¼ teaspoons (7 g) gelatin mass (⅜ teaspoon/1 g gelatin powder hydrated in 1¼ teaspoons/6 g water)
- 1½ teaspoons (10 g) candied orange paste
- 1½ teaspoons (10 g) candied lemon paste
- 3½ tablespoons (50 g) rum

In a saucepan, combine ⅞ cup (205 g) water with the sugar, gelatin mass, and candied orange and lemon and heat. Filter through a conical sieve and add the rum.

iNDEX

BY

iNGREDiENT

BiOS

YOHANN CARON

2008
- Retrained as a pastry chef after five years as a culinary chef
- Trained at Frédérick Fossey, Moulins

2011
- First meeting with Cédric Grolet and joined the team at Le Meurice hotel as a demi chef de partie

2013
- Pastry sous chef at Le Meurice

2017
- Birth of his son, Paul

2018
- Assistant executive pastry chef for the opening of the pastry boutique at Le Meurice

2019
- Executive pastry chef at Opéra bakery-pâtisserie

FRANÇOIS DESHAYES

2011-2012
- Vocational diploma in cooking at Metz, with honors

2013
- Speciality diploma in restaurant desserts

2014
- Pastry commis chef at Le Meurice

2016
- Demi chef de partie at Le Meurice

2018
- Pastry sous chef at Le Meurice

2019
- Assistant executive pastry chef under Cédric Grolet at Le Meurice

2000

Starts vocational training to become a pastry chef

2006

Becomes a commis chef at Fauchon

2011

Becomes a sous chef at Hôtel Le Meurice

2013

Promoted to executive pastry chef at Hôtel Le Meurice

2015

Recognized as pastry chef of the year by *Le Chef* magazine

2016

Wins the Relais Desserts Prix d'Excellence for pastry chef of the year

Wins the Toques Blanches pastry chef of the year award

2017

Recognized as pastry chef of the year by Omnivore

His first book, *Fruits*, is published by Ducasse Édition

2018

Opens the Hôtel Le Meurice pastry boutique, rue de Castiglione, Paris

Recognized as best pastry chef in the world by Grandes Tables du Monde

2019

Opens the Opéra bakery-pâtisserie, avenue de l'Opéra in Paris

His second book, *Opéra*, is published by Ducasse Édition

Chosen best pastry chef in the world by the World's 50 Best Restaurants

2021-2022

Opens his first store in London "Cédric Grolet The Berkeley"

His third book, *Fleurs*, is published by Ducasse Édition

Rubik's Flower ❀ Available to order from Cédric Grolet Opéra,
35, avenue de l'Opéra, 75002 Paris.

Thank you to **FRANKA HOLTMANN**, general manager of Le Meurice, for your unwavering support. ● Thank you to **ALAiN DUCASSE** for the wonderful times we've shared. ● Thank you to **YOHANN CARON** & **FRANÇOiS DESHAYES**, my two exectutive chefs. Nothing would be possible without you. ● Thank you to all **MY TEAMS** at Opéra and Le Meurice for all your support throughout the making of this book. ● Thank you to **LESLiE GOGOiS** & **HENRY ASSELiN** for your steady presence on the ground. ● Thank you to atelier **LOUiS DEL BOCA** for the creativity that goes into your work, which practically mirrors our own. ● Thank you to the talented **CALViN COURJON** for your photos. ● Thank you to **MAiSON COLOM** for providing me with high-quality fruit. ● Thank you to **SOiNS GRAPHiQUES**, and more particularly to Aurélie Mansion and Pierre Tachon, for your talent and your incredible design work for this book. ● Thank you to Éditions Alain Ducasse for your trust, and thank you to **JULiE DEFFONTAiNES** for your involvement. ● Thank you to **RĒMi TESSiER** for your invaluable contacts and advice. ● Thank you to **ALiCiA**, "my guardian angel." ● A special thank you to **ASTRiD OLiViA**.

COLLECTION DIRECTOR
Alain Ducasse

MANAGING DIRECTOR
Aurore Charoy

EDITORIAL MANAGER
Julie Deffontaines

ART DIRECTION,
GRAPHIC DESIGN,
LAYOUT
Soins Graphiques
Pierre Tachon, Camille Demaimay,
and Aurélie Mansion

TEXT
Leslie Gogois

TRANSLATION
Cillero & De Motta

COPY EDITOR
Sarah Scheffel

PHOTOGRAPHY
Calvin Courjon

Printed in China
ISBN: 978-2-37945-082-2
Legal deposit 3rd quarter 2023

Distributed in North America
by ABRAMS, New York.

© Ducasse Édition 2021
2, rue Paul Vaillant-Couturier
92532 Levallois Perret Cedex, France